A MOVING EXPERIENCE

Dance for Lovers of Children
and the Child Within

Teresa Benzwie, Ph.D.

Illustrated by Robert Bender

Zephyr Press

Tucson, Arizona

About the artist—

Robert Bender is a graduate of Syracuse University School of Visual Arts
where he was the recipient of the Senior Faculty Merit Award for illustration.
His promotional and editorial work has been featured in various magazines
and publications. He now resides in New York City as a free-lance illustrator.

A Moving Experience
Dance for Lovers of Children

Grades PreK–6

Copyright © 1987, Teresa Benzwie
Second Printing, 1988

Printed in the United States of America

ISBN 0-913705-25-X

Published by Zephyr Press, Tucson, Arizona

Zephyr Press
P.O. Box 66006
Tucson, Arizona 85728-6006

DEDICATION

This book is lovingly dedicated to
my three beautiful sons

Lawrence

Craig

Robert

who have been a constant joy
and inspiration to me.

CONTENTS

PRELUDE

This book is an outgrowth of my experiences in the classroom and my lifelong love of children and dance. It stems from my belief that children need to move, create, and value themselves as respected, loving human beings who have something distinctively their own to celebrate.

The seeds for my ideas and beliefs were planted a long time ago in my own childhood. We were expected to passively absorb teacher-initiated information from behind our desks, while our natural energies and zest for life were either repressed or interpreted as misbehavior. As an active child, I often escaped into daydreaming and fantasy, using expressive movement to feel good about myself and the world.

As an adult, I have brought forth my fantasy and expressive movement abilities to teaching, where curriculum is primary. Learning basic skills and being academically prepared for the next grade were and still are top priorities. Creative movement as a modality helps us gain knowledge through the body and grasp the essence of learning from within, connecting to ourselves in the deepest, most direct ways. Movement helps to bridge differences that are sometimes associated with age, size, sex, or abilities. These individual differences can then be celebrated, affirmed, and developed. Through movement, our bodies connect with the world of abstraction and our dreams to the world of possible reality. As the world changes, the arts, of which creative movement is one, persist and fulfill our lives.

Today, my well-developed ability to fantasize and to use dance has become a powerful teaching tool, helping me build magical worlds where children are fully valued for their ability to give and receive.

A book may be written by one person, but many others' involvement in its creation brings it to life. The heart of *A Moving Experience* beats strongly because of the contributions and responses of many educators, artists, and children.

Dr. Edrie Ferdun, professor of Dance at Temple University, my doctoral advisor and mentor, guided and enriched my life professionally and personally. She is a rare individual who can see the potential in others and support and nurture them from a powerful place within her own psyche.

My son, Robert Bender, created the inspired and sensitive illustrations. As a child, Robert would visit my kindergarten classes and in high school he began to sketch my students. He brings a connectedness and understanding to my work that would not be available from any other artist. Together we danced and worked with the children in the illustrations. Thank you, Robert, for capturing their spirit on these pages. It has been a joy to watch your talent emerge and actualize.

Dr. Harlene Galen, an extraordinary person, woman of generous spirit, dear friend and principal of the Magowan School in Edgewater Park, New Jersey, provided quiet strength and understanding friendship. Despite a busy schedule, she found time to help me from the first editing stages to this book's publication. Her spirit and school energized and inspired me.

Joan Lawrence Lavine, Sheila Greenberg, JoAnn White and Deborah Curtiss provided inspiration, editing skills and loving time. Emerson Darnell gave generously of his friendship and legal expertise.

Maria Caterino tested *A Moving Experience* with her physical education classes at Red Bank School, New Jersey, with fascinating results. Walter J. Dold, Edgewater Park, New Jersey Superintendent of Schools, shared his school facilities to support dance education. Dorothy Maron, a genuinely good sport, always welcomed my movement endeavors to her third and fourth grade classes; and Susan Conner permitted her first grade youngsters to take part in my ongoing explorations.

Joey Tanner and the staff at Zephyr Press caught the vision and with love and dedication, launched *A Moving Experience* into reality.

Finally, the wonderful children from my kindergarten classes in Camden, New Jersey, 1968-1984, provided the inspiration for me to share this work. They contributed an excitement for learning and wholeheartedly trusted the experience of using their minds, bodies and feelings. Together we explored, developed and totally invested ourselves in the movement adventures.

To all, my most sincere personal thanks, hugs, and gratitude.

Teresa Benzwie

Teresa Benzwie

FOREWORD

Dancing can remind adults of who they are, or were, or wanted to be . . . fully alive, breathing participants in a dramatic world of contour, color, rhythm, motion, and much more. Teresa Benzwie never forgets the possibilities of dancing. She remembers the deep need she and the children she teaches have to celebrate and to change in the same activities. She carries the reminder to us in this loving book which tells and shows what it means to reinstate children and teachers as prime movers, creators, and collaborators in the business of the school.

The realization that dancing is compatible with social responsibility and mature authority on the part of teachers is an important contribution of the book. In many ways, the stress symptoms and disorders in learning, eating, and social control now seen in the young point to the increasing necessity for teachers to provide a positive ground of bodily experience, perceptual organization, and human connection, such as can be achieved in dance activity. Children need to be in situations where the flow of their sensation and sense of significance is not only relevant but guided and valued as it is formed.

Mostly, children need a fully present adult who has an unquestionable commitment to them as sensitive, active individuals and developing members of a caring community. Readers need such an author as well, and in this book, have one, in Teresa Benzwie who shares the values, attitudes, materials and skills she has developed in her exceptional career as a teacher. She promotes achievement in all of us by encouraging us to keep hopes and fantasy alive. For the reality of Teresa Benzwie as a person, friend, teacher, film maker, now author, and always dancer, I am deeply grateful and inspired.

Edrie Ferdun, PhD
Professor of Dance
Temple University
Philadelphia, PA

Learning is:
A Moving Experience

"We all need to experience the freedom and joy
  of our own creative movement.
It makes no difference what age, size, sex,
  or what condition our bodies are in.
The feelings are the same
  in all of us.
We need to create, to express and be nourished
  as we learn from experiences which connect
  to our deepest selves.

There is no one
  who can be and dance like any other.
We all have our own genius
  when we allow it to emerge:

To be ourselves
  and to create;
To again capture the feeling of the child within us,
  along with our adult understanding;
And to allow that child to feel
  full freedom of expression.

We give this special gift
  of ourselves to our children:
We appreciate their individual beauty
  and create an environment and goals for them,
So that they can direct their natural high energy
  for constructive, creative and fulfilling lives."

The more we know about education and how the brain processes information, the more we understand that movement is central to learning. However, we often tend to immobilize children behind desks instead of utilizing the potential of their tremendous natural vitality. To understand symbols such as numerals and letters, or ideas in science and social studies, children can use not only eyes and ears, but the entire being. How far is far and how near is near is experienced from the perspective of the child's own body. Through such relatedness, abstractions become more concrete, and learning becomes an internal process.

Beginning in infancy, the progression from dependence to independence is based on being able to move: from turning over, to reaching for objects, to crawling, to walking. In schools, teachers enhance this process. We CAN use this inherent necessity to move, the desire for self-expression and independence to enrich learning in all areas of the curriculum.

The beauty of using creative movement as a method of teaching is that it not only helps children to learn cognitive skills from concrete and personal experiences, it also stimulates and encourages them to reach their highest potential.

The following exercises and ideas enable both teachers and children to find new ways for their bodies to move. Each of us has something unique and wonderful that is ours alone . . . something special that only we can be and offer to others. To come to know our own special genius is a lifetime process. A significant manifestation of this specialness is our body moving . . . in finding our own dance. Out of these movement exercises, a wholistic learning environment evolves, one which is supportive of the attitude that each of us is appreciated, acknowledged, and respected for who we are.

Movement exploration is important in problem-solving. For example, questions or tasks can be approached in as many or more ways as there are students in a room. The belief that the teacher knows THE answer, and that some child will be able to verbalize it, blocks real thinking. By contrast, creative problem-solving is open to new ways of doing things, untried possibilities and different strategies. With this approach, children probe, think, and succeed, becoming an integral and organic force in the classroom.

On a social level, children learn to work cooperatively with each other. As the teacher reinforces the students' personal growth, they learn to support and encourage one another. Children begin to appreciate individual effort, value positive thinking and nurture mutual respect. This atmosphere fosters spontaneity, leadership, and self-control.

Another aspect of creative movement is aesthetics: the "Ahhhhh, it feels so good to move, to create, to dance!" With the freedom to improvise, many beautiful dances are created spontaneously. These are the precious moments for which a teacher lives, the moments we wish we could capture "for always."

The exercises that follow have been developed for the classroom. Although your space may seem crowded, and open areas at a premium, one can maximize the space by re-arranging desks either in close groups, or in a large open square. Many activities can be done while students sit at the desk, stand in the aisle or face partners. Whatever space there is, movement is possible.

The teacher is also a participant, working and dancing with the children. The child receives a nonverbal message; "It's OK to work this way . . . I'm doing it too. It's OK to risk being different or feeling silly. We are all learning together." When we share the same space as we move, we can develop considerate, gentle communication and non-verbal group sensitivity. The teacher develops rapport with the children and both intellectually and intuitively, gains a better understanding of their needs, frustrations and potential.

Creative movement is a natural process of total involvement and could be initiated by asking, "How could I use my body to reinforce any given concept? How can I use space to introduce this mathematics problem? How can I involve the students physically, mentally and socially as we deal with daily challenges?" As the teacher becomes accustomed to using bodies in space as a tool for learning, answers begin to come more easily. And children, a boundless source of ideas, contribute generously to the learning process.

Begin with simple activities. The more you participate and feel comfortable, the more your freedom of expression grows, and the more spontaneous and creative the children will become.

As you read **A Moving Experience**, you will be able to hear me talking to the children. My words will be guiding them in the kinds of moving experiences we have created together year after year in the classroom. You will see the children responding to the challenge, fantasy, love and support of the lessons through the illustrations provided by Robert Bender. I encourage you to hear your own voice and imagine your own students moving, dancing, and learning. My suggestions and comments, in bold type, are meant to be a sharing between us. By writing down your ideas as well, the power of the book will grow.

You may begin anywhere. The order of contents and sequences is not fixed. The movement ideas are open-ended so that the experiences reinforce each other.

I see you, the teacher, as a facilitator, providing a rich, stimulating environment, giving guidance and positive support. Creative movement enriches this process. Students are embarking on an adventure of continuous learning about themselves, each other, and the universe in which they live.

In creative movement, there is no set or specific way to move, to dance, to be. Every way is THE way.

Teresa Benzwie

INTRODUCTION

We, as individuals, are as different from each other as snowflakes, and each of us, especially in childhood, explores the world in different ways.

In order to preserve the genius and developmental potential of childhood, we teachers and caretakers must give the universe back to the child, and we must do so in as rich and dramatic a form as possible.

How we function is determined by the extent to which we use our whole organism at any time and in any situation. When we use it fully and efficiently, we succeed in the larger sense of approaching our own potential.

Educators, teachers, and parents will become much more effective in their relations with children by integrating areas of the classroom curriculum with movement and feelings. As we encourage the education of the whole brain and the whole child, we establish a learning environment where children can feel good about themselves and respect and support each other.

Learning, then, becomes a synergistic context of head and heart, thinking and action . . . "back to basics" at its very best . . . the basics of learning how to learn.

Dr. Jean Houston, Psychologist
Director, Foundation for Mind Research, Pomona, New York
Author, *The Possible Human*

RANGE

Most any small movement exploration can become a fuller more involved lesson by expanding the movement to include:

> *individual body parts, to the use of the entire body.*
>
> *movement in the sitting, lying, and standing positions.*
>
> *moving in place, to using the entire space.*
>
> *working alone, to moving with a partner, with small groups and with the entire group.*
>
> *different locomotor movements.*
>
> *highly structured, to spontaneous free movement.*

DEVELOPING RANGE OF MOVEMENT

BEGIN SIMPLY AND BUILD ON IT
Finger plays which are used in most kindergarten classrooms can become a dance experience. Fingers and hands "act out" songs and rhymes such as "Open-Shut Them."

"Open-shut them, open-shut them,
give a little clap.
Open-shut them, open-shut them,
Place them in your lap."

What other body part can you open and close? Your arms! Good! Let's everyone do it. What other body part can you open and close? Your shoulders! Show us . . . . Now everyone do it. Wonderful! What other body part? . . . . nose . . . . legs . . . . eyes . . . . neck . . . . mouth . . .
Or whatever else the children suggest. And they do propose some unusual ideas. If you can't figure out how the nose or neck can open or close just ask the children. They usually have a way.

Now the whole body. Let's find a way to open and close our whole body from a standing position.

That's wonderful! Look at all the different ways you are finding to open and close your body.

Using Creative Problem Solving, children can find their own body part to move and a different way to open and close.

No problem has only one solution. Thus, each problem provides opportunities to succeed, to be right in different ways. As children contribute to the lesson, their interest is aroused and they soon become integral parts of a creative experience.

In slow motion, let's all stretch our bodies as open as we can and make ourselves very wide and tall. Ohhhh, that feels so good, such a nice stretch!

Now, also in slow motion, begin to close yourselves in. Finally, make yourself end up in a tight, small ball low down on the floor. Feel every body part closing . . . . fingers, toes, stomach, head, all of you.

Open-Close Dance

Good! Now I will put on some music and you may open and close your bodies in your own time and create your own open and close dance.

Each time you open or close, find a new position and a new way to do it. Opening and closing. Stretching and curling in slow motion. Experience how good it feels to find your very own positions, your very own dance.

Use as much of the space as possible without touching anyone else. We want you to have the freedom for your beautiful dance and also respect each other's work. Be aware of the empty spaces to move into and try not to get in each others' way.

Turn to the person nearest you and try your dance together . . . . a cooperative dance of open and close. With a partner you can find new ways to move.

Keep it nonverbal. Your bodies can talk for you. Give each other messages with your bodies. Keep exploring new ways to move together in an open and close dance . . . .

Now two groups of two get together and become a group of four. Don't hold on to each other during your dance, just touch, gently finding ways to work together.

Remember to keep it nonverbal. Listen to the music, finding new positions, new shapes to show open and closed. Freeze the final open and close position for a moment and admire yourselves . . . . You're beautiful!

Now two groups of four get together and become a group of eight. Can you find a new way to cooperate in such a large group?

Let me see you create an open position. Some of you may be low, down near the floor and some of you are high. All of you are as open as you can be. Oh! They are beautiful shapes. Now let's try a closed shape. Good!

Now to the music. Using your own timing, the entire group of eight will create an open-close dance . . . . Slowly stretching on different levels, opening up to each other, touching gently.

And now begin to close your bodies off from each other. Closed to yourselves only . . . . And now again open to the group. Sometimes we want to be open to each other and to the outside world and sometimes we need to close off from the world.

Create your group open-close dance. Feel openness. Feel its opposite . . . . closed. Be aware of each other. Everyone opening and closing. Slowly use the entire space and each other to open and close.

This lesson can be stopped at any point depending on time and class needs.

Opposites

round-straight
    sit-stand
small-large
    freeze-melt
push-pull
    wide-narrow
left-right
    hot-cold
        fast-slow
           near-far
       sad-happy
         up-down
      light-strong
        under-over
     yes-no
       in-out
     tall-short
       loud-soft

You name some more.

Let your opposites
become a dance.
**Ask students how they
feel about their dance
and which of the
opposites they prefer.**

**Some of these opposites may be
very therapeutic: "Push all
your cares away", "Pull towards
you all the good things you
want."**

**Practice "Yes-No" with
assertiveness and
determination.**

**Maria Caterino, physical education teacher from New Jersey, added sound to this
experience with her second-grade classes. The drum and slide whistle worked very
well with the opposites "freeze-melt".**

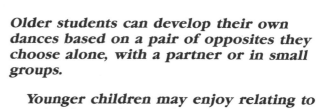

Older students can develop their own dances based on a pair of opposites they choose alone, with a partner or in small groups.

Younger children may enjoy relating to animals or objects that are big-small, soft-hard, etc.

Always leave room for experiences that will spontaneously arise from the children.

9

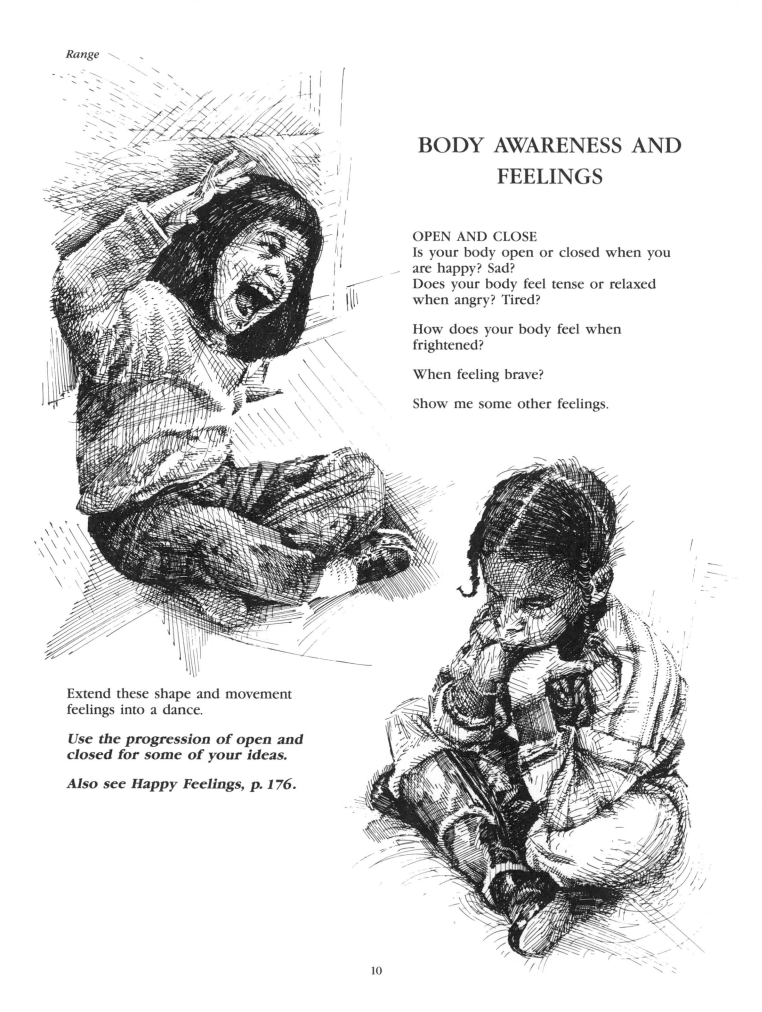

BODY AWARENESS AND FEELINGS

OPEN AND CLOSE
Is your body open or closed when you are happy? Sad?
Does your body feel tense or relaxed when angry? Tired?

How does your body feel when frightened?

When feeling brave?

Show me some other feelings.

Extend these shape and movement feelings into a dance.

Use the progression of open and closed for some of your ideas.

Also see Happy Feelings, p. 176.

Opening

AS IN A GIFT, A FLOWER OR YOURSELF
In Partners:
One partner, curl yourself up as tightly as possible.
The other partner, very slowly uncurl your partner
until he is totally aligned. Pick up the legs by the
ankles and lightly shake them, getting the hips
straightened as you do. Do the same for the arms.

Ask your partner if he feels straight.

Change roles. Share feelings of how it
felt to be opened and all stretched
out. How did you feel as closed?

What else happened that you would
like to share?

**Poldi Orlando, Gestalt and Dance
Therapist, had us experience
"Opening" in one of her many
workshops for the Association for
Humanistic Psychology.**

SPACE

We all relate to space differently. Some of us need a great deal of room while others enjoy close proximity. Our feelings on how much distance we need will change depending on where we are, whom we're with or how we feel at that moment.

Learning to work together cooperatively in mutual space is an ongoing experience. To appreciate the spatial needs of others, we must know our own needs and be sensitive to the boundary cues which we and others give.

EXPLORING SPACE

DISCUSSION

While sitting in the space you're in, look around the room. How do you feel about the room? How does the room make **you** feel? What signs tell you the room is for children? Adults? Does this room have a special use? Is the room warm and comfortable or cold and unfriendly? What is dominant? What about the room creates these feelings?

The purpose of the following questions is to promote mental rather than verbal responses.

Explore the entire room with your body. Find spaces you can fit into. Become aware of the spaces. Are they round or straight? What shape does your body have to make to fit into these spaces? Try different body parts in the same space. Explore . . . . Find new ways to explore on a low level. Try crawling, slithering, rolling . . . . Find other ways to be on a medium level . . . . on a high level . . . . Do you see new shapes and spaces to explore from this perspective?

Lie on your back and look up at the ceiling and other parts of the room. What shapes and spaces do you see? Crawl under chairs : . . . over tables.

Can you go into anything?

Find all the corners, nooks and crannies. The little places—the larger ones. Notice how the room takes on a different perspective from
    A lying down position,
        A sitting position,
            Or a standing position.

Space exploration is more fun in a classroom where there is furniture to explore. If this is done in a gym, you may want to put some equipment around, to create spaces.

This experience is done nonverbally with nonmelodic music used as background sound.

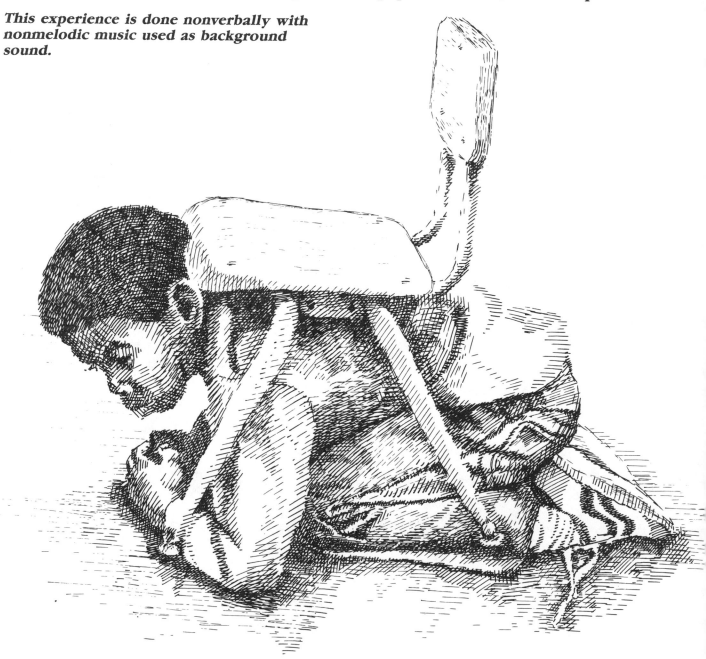

Your Space

Find the place in the room where you feel
most comfortable. Go there now.

Notice where you are.
> Are you near a wall, a corner,
> Near the middle of the room?
> Are you up high on top of something,
> Near the floor or under something?
> Do you have your back to,
> Or are you facing the rest of the group?
> Are you hidden?
> Can you be seen?
> What is the range of your vision?
> Are you leaning against or on something,
> Or are you in the middle of the space?

> This can also be done in your home.
> > Which is your favorite room?
> > > Chair?
> > > > Side of the bed?
> Ask yourself why.
> You might find new comfortable places
> by exploring your own home.

*I remember a workshop with Christopher Beck,
dance therapist and performer, in which we explored
an entire house with our bodies. In this interesting way we
discovered much about the place we would dance in.*

Finding Your Spot

Walk around the room until you find your favorite spot. You may then sit or stand on it. Give
it your name. Write it with your finger (or other body part) on the floor.

> Be aware of:
> > Who is on your right, left, in back of you and in front of you.
> > How far away you are from the door, window or furniture.
> > What you are standing on or under.

One at a time call out your place with your name. Run to another place in the room.
Skip back. Did you get back to your same spot? Check your landmarks!

Continue with other locomotor movements, varying them with
slowly	*smoothly*
quickly	*low*
high	*and so on.*

SHARING THOUGHTS
How do you feel about the room now?
Is there a change? Do you feel more comfortable?
Is the room more familiar?
What do you know about the room now that you didn't know before?
What part of the room was your favorite, or the place you were most comfortable in? Why?

How did you feel doing this experience?
What problems arose?
How were they worked out?
What new shapes did you find?
Where were they?

How is space divided or used in your home, school or other places?

This experience is for all ages. The older the students, the more sophisticated the awareness will be. It may also be used to become familiar with a new space.

Walking into or sitting in a room may give us a limited perspective. Crawling or lying down can reveal a different view. Just as in ALICE IN WONDERLAND, we find spaces we didn't know existed before. Maybe you'll find new places to crawl into to be alone with a book or some quiet thoughts. Rooms that are crowded can be stretched with imagination.

Remember how you sometimes like to find those out of the way places to hide in or under so you can observe the world in a different way, creating your own fantasies? This is our chance to relive those fantasies, create new ones and make this room belong to you.

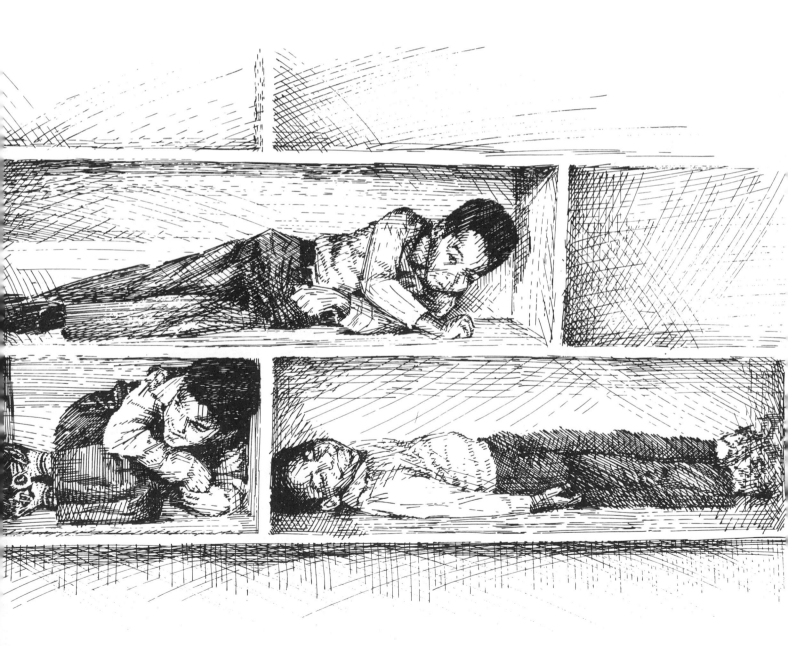

EXPLORING SPACE THROUGH OTHER SENSES

Exploring space can be limited to the use of just one of the senses.

Be aware of texture. Close your eyes. How does the rug, floor, furniture, etc. feel to your hands, arms, cheek or the bottoms of your feet? Are they hard or soft, rough or smooth? Be aware of change of textures as you move from one place to another.

Be aware of sounds. Run your fingers across a grating or tap the object you are exploring.

Find all the spaces in the room that are round and that are straight.

After a spontaneous exploration you may want to structure the lesson more by exploring a specific shape or object such as a chair or hoop.

Find one object in the room that you want to stay with and explore more intensely.

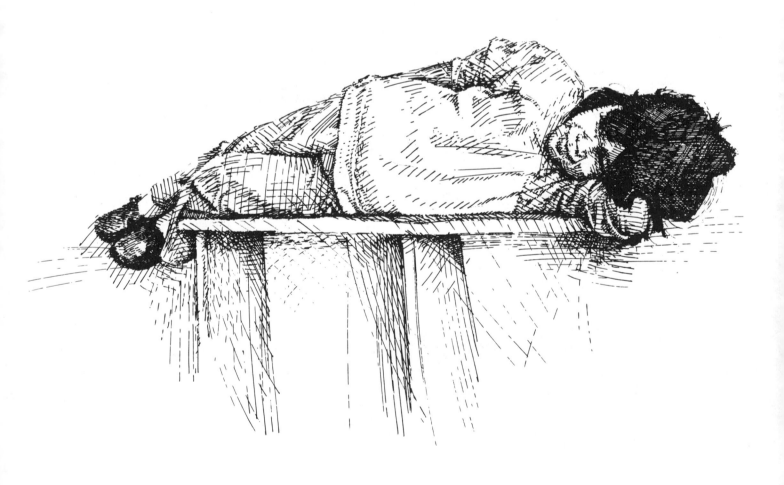

PERSONAL SPACE

Your personal space is all the space you are in and can reach while being in a stationary position at any given time.

Sit in a space by yourself far enough away from anyone else so you cannot touch them. Slowly reach out and explore all the space around you, in front, behind, next to, above and underneath you. Now use your legs to do the same.

Stretch these parts of your body in all possible positions, one at a time, alternating, both together, over your head, to the side, crossing over. Find new ways to stretch. Now slowly get yourself to a standing position. Keeping your feet stationary, stretch your arms and body in all directions. Explore all the space around you.

Asking children to find their own personal space is a helpful beginning for many lessons.

PERSONAL
SPACE
STRETCH
DANCE

Find your personal space.
Begin in a lying down position.
Close your eyes and visualize which of
your body parts want to stretch . . . .
Slowly open your eyes and allow your
body to stretch, one movement leading
into the other. Your body will tell you what
part it wants to stretch next. Slowly evolve
to a sitting position and then to standing.
Continue your slow motion stretch . . . .
one continuous flow. Allow twisting and
bending to help you stretch. Keep your feet
as stationary as possible.

*Teacher participation,
teacher acceptance, and
use of children's ideas
can help sustain the
attention span.*

SPACE FLOW

Experience ongoing movement, creating spaces and shapes as you involve your whole body: bending, twisting, and flowing in relationship to your partner. Your partner will be flowing in and out of your shapes while simultaneously creating her own spaces as she moves. This is an ongoing dance of moving and flowing in and out of the ever changing shapes and negative spaces of your partner. *See Negative-Positive Spaces, p. 130.*

Try this in small groups of three or four. There can also be many changes of partners, flowing from one to another. This can be used for a group to begin to know each other.

SPACE AWARENESS GAMES

Opposing Circles

Form two circles, one inside the other. One circle of people will be walking to the left, the other to the right. Walk in time to a beat *(clapping or drumbeat)*, always keeping the spaces between you and the person in front and back of you equal.

There needs to be the same amount of space evenly divided between each person in both circles.

When you are tapped or your name is called, move to the other circle. Then everyone will re-adjust the spacing to be even again.

This can go on for awhile, inside people moving to outside circle and vice-versa. You can also use other locomotor movements such as marching, hopping or jumping.

Your Name and Desired Space

Say your name continuously. As you say your name, use your arms and hands to shape the desired space you want or need right now. You might feel very closed and want a very small space, so you will trace a space close to your body. You might feel expansive and need a great deal of space. You then might carve out a large space in the room. You may want to include other people in your space, or close them out.

Allow time to verbally share feelings.

Sensitivity Circle Walk

This is good for larger groups of at least fifteen people.

Make as large a circle as possible, but do not hold hands. One person go into the center, and close your eyes. Begin walking in any direction. The circle of people will protect you. If you walk to the edge someone will gently turn you back to face the center. Try walking at different speeds, quickly as well as slowly. Make sure your eyes stay closed.

A great deal of trust is required.

As a variation, the circle of people can use sound as the person in the center approaches the edge. The closest person can make any type of sound to warn the person in the middle to change direction.

Larger and Smaller

Imagine that you are growing larger. Take up as much space as you can. How do you feel taking up a lot of space? When is it possible in your real life to do this?

Make yourself as small as you can . . . . How does this feel? Under what circumstances have you taken up only a small amount of space?

When you enter a room what do you usually do, take up a lot or a little space? Which do you prefer?

Inside a Box

Imagine you are inside a box. Take some time and feel the ceiling. Now feel all four walls and now the floor. How large is your box? How do you feel inside this box? How does your body fit into it?

Feel comfortable!
Your box protects you.

Your box is your prison!
Break out any way you can.

Discuss your feelings of being in limited space.

See Fantasy Environments, p. 157.

25

MOVING THROUGH SPACE CONSTRUCTIVELY

You ask, "How do you get children to move through space without bumping into each other, getting wild or knocking each other down?" Well, it does need to be worked on because it doesn't usually happen by itself.

Using the entire room, let's see if you can move through the space without touching each other. Good! Let's move faster, faster . . . . Freeze! Very good! Now let's move in slow motion. Can you move very slowly without touching each other? Very good!

We will now make the space we are moving in smaller. Let's see if you can move quickly in this smaller space without touching each other. Very good! Can you go even faster? Freeze! . . . Now again in slow motion. Very good!

If one child is being disruptive such as pushing, shoving, falling or sprawling on the floor, I will move alongside this child, encouraging him in a positive way. There are usually no more than one or two children who need this special attention.

When any lesson is not working well or the students are not being cooperative, you could stop the lesson, and work on the particular problem by itself. This may take only five minutes and then you are ready to return to the original lesson.

MEASURING SPACE

Measure the length or width of the room or piece of furniture or space between objects with different body parts or your total body.

Example: "This table is five arm lengths long."

Using locomotor movements, find how many
　　　　walks,
　　　　　skips,
　　　　　　hops, etc.
it takes to cross the length of this room.

How many steps does it take to measure this ladder?

RHYTHM

All life has a rhythm:

   The seasons
      The singing of the birds
         The cycle of the moon
            A New York City street
               The rain
                  Day and night
                     Our pulse, breathing, heartbeat and
                        The individual ways we move.

Learning has a rhythm also. Some learn quickly, some more slowly, some take it in more deeply.
   Some auditorily,
      Visually or
         Kinesthetically.
            Each has its rhythm.

Certain skills need to be learned by rote, such as the letters of the alphabet and the multiplication tables. Learning by rote with rhythm gives the process life.

MOVING TO NUMBER FOUR

Close your eyes and listen to how
many times I clap my hands. 1-2-3-4.
Good! . . . . four times.
Now open your eyes and we'll all clap
four times together, 1-2-3-4.

Tap each other's shoulders gently four
times.

Shrug your shoulders four times. 1-2-3-4.

What else can you move four times?
Good!

*Continue asking the students what other body
parts they can move four times, or how else
they can move them. I am constantly delighted
at the variety and uniqueness of ideas the
children bring to the lesson. The variations are
limitless.*

Scrunch your nose four times, 1-2-3-4.
Shake your head four times, 1-2-3-4.
Punch the air four times, 1-2-3-4.
Kick your legs four times, 1-2-3-4.
Raise your legs up and down four times, 1-2-3-4.
Open and close your eyes four times.
Wonderful! What else?

Now let's rise slowly to the count of four. Can you
take four steps in any direction? *Try stamping,
jumping, turning, kicking, hopping, etc.*

Take four steps into an empty space and freeze in a
sculpture on the fourth count. See if you can do this
without touching anybody else. 1-2-3-freeze. Let's try
again. Look around to see where an empty space is,
and don't get too close to furniture or to the sides of
the room. Now take four steps into the space, freezing
on the fourth count. Good!

You may need to change your direction in order not to touch anybody else.
Again . . . .Ready . . . . Together . . . . 1-2-3-freeze.

Look at all the beautiful sculptures! They're all so different!

*Encourage movement away from each other. Young children tend to bunch together
instead of using open space.*

This time when we freeze, we will end up on a high level. Ready, 1-2-3-freeze . . . .
Good! . . . . again, 1-2-3-freeze.

Now on a low level. Let's see how many different sculptures you can make on a low
level . . . . without touching anybody else.

1-2-3-freeze . . . Good! They're beautiful!

Now, let's try an in-between level!
      Not too high . . . .
        Not too low . . . .
Just in-between or medium.
         Oh, they are wonderful!

Now, we will count again and move 1-2-3-freeze on a medium level.
      Great! . . . . Again!
        1-2-3-freeze . . . . Again!

Now, we will combine them. 1-2-3-freeze high.
      1-2-3-freeze on a low level.
        1-2-3-freeze on a medium level.

Now, you decide. On what level do you want to freeze? Some of you will end up on a high
level, some low, and some will be on a medium level. All different levels.
      Let's begin 1-2-3-freeze.
        Beautiful!
      They all look so interesting . . . . Again . . . .
        Change your level. 1-2-3-4 . . . .

Continue a few more times, encouraging students to change their level each time.

This time when we freeze, we will gently touch someone near us. 1-2-3-touch.
    Good! Is everyone attached to someone?
    (Erik) is touching (Cynthia's) shoulder.
    (Carl) is touching (Tamika's) back.
See if you can find another body part to touch with. Good!
You're using your hips
          feet
            shoulders
             elbows
              head.

What interesting sculptures! Let's try it again.
1-2-3-touch. Good! Again!

CHANGING AND COMBINING LEVELS

1-2-3-freeze. Touching on a high level.
1-2-3-freeze. Touching on a low level.
1-2-3-freeze. Touching on a medium level.

Now, let's combine them again. Some high, some low and some on a medium level, always touching. Change your level each time you freeze.
Begin! 1-2-3-4 . . . . Don't forget to touch.

Continue this as long as attention span lasts. It's visually very effective. You can also make it a dance. The last part of this lesson lends itself to some free improvisation.

At any point, the lesson can stop in order to concentrate on a particular theme. For example:
Let's explore all the possible ways we can create a sculpture on a medium level. Experiment with touching gently with different body parts. Let's see if we can move around the room rhythmically without touching. *See p. 27.* Let's practice freezing on the count of four, and holding it before we go on.

There may be other points of difficulty or areas that need practice before you continue further into your lesson. A set amount of time is not neccessary. Each teacher needs to realize the rhythm for her own individual classes.

FOR OLDER STUDENTS
CREATE OTHER COMBINATIONS OF NUMBERS
With partners alternating, first person, create eight distinct movements. Next partner respond with eight movements of your own, and so on with 4-2-and 1.

Enjoy a communication with your partner based on 8-4-2-1.

Create your own rhythmic dance, using a combination of rhythms such as 1-3-1-3. One can be a slow movement and then three quick movements. You make up other combinations for your dance.

The rest of the class will learn the rhythm, and accompany the dance with rhythmic instruments.

DANCE OF NUMBER NINE

Create many combinations of one number, such as;

3-3-3

2-2-1-2-2

4-1-4

We will dance the combinations of nine. Form groups of nine. Each group create a sculpture connecting on different levels. Yes, you are now a sculpture of nine. Now dance away and freeze again, spontaneously dividing and breaking up the group of nine into smaller groups such as 1-1-4-3 . . . Now dance back into your whole group, connecting again. Continue this dance of breaking up into smaller combinations of nine, and coming back to one group again. Let's see how many different combinations of nine you can make.

Vary the movements away and to the whole by changing the quality.
Move in a slithering manner,
    jagged,
        sustained (uninterrupted),
            quickly,
                slowly.
                    You make up some more.

A DANCE OF EIGHT COUNTS

One person will create a movement for the first count of eight. Someone else keep adding on his movements until we have a choreography to the count of eight. We will repeat this in different variations such as: quickly, slowly, strong, light, with different types of music: sad, elegant, nervous, etc.

PASSING A BALL AROUND IN A CIRCLE

Rhythmically pass a ball around with music.

Vary it with:
Saying the multiplication tables
   Counting by ones, fives, tens, etc.
      Adding, and so on.

In groups of 20 you may have as many as 10 balls being passed around. Vary the passing by . . . .

Touch both knees before passing it on,
   both feet,
      both shoulders.

Find other ways to pass the balls.
When you get the ball
   Say your name,
      Or your address,
         Or your birthday,
            Or your favorite color,
               What else can you say?

WALKING ON DIFFERENT NUMBERS OF BODY PARTS

How can you walk on four body parts? Can you show me a different way? Another way? Walk on three body parts . . . . six . . . . . Can you do it differently? Wonderful!

Look at all the different ways you can walk on five body parts.

BODY RHYTHMS

What is your rhythm in the morning? Do you jump out of bed immediately? Do you just turn over and lie a few minutes longer? Can you communicate early or only after breakfast, or possibly noon? Who will volunteer to reinact his morning routine?

Silently show us how your body feels from the moment you open your eyes until you leave for school or play. Visualize the moments and allow your body to remember how it is as you go through your morning ritual.

Compare rhythms with each other. Who was faster? Slower? Did some speed up or slow down as you proceeded throughout the morning? Did some keep a consistent rhythm?

Would you like to try and change your morning rhythm? If you do, how would you be able to? One way would be to get up earlier to give more time. What are some other ways?

This can be altered somewhat for a lesson on personal hygiene, bathing, balanced breakfast, exercise etc.

Your rhythms may change from morning to evening; from one activity to another; or from weekend to weekday.

How can a holiday or crisis make a difference in your rhythm?

How do seasons or weather conditions affect rhythms? What are some other factors that will affect your rhythm?

RHYTHM OF YOUR NAME

We're going to say hello to each other, listening for each syllable and clapping it.

H E L – L O — M E – L I N – D A

Let's say and clap each child's name without saying hello and count how many syllables each one has.

If there are mistakes, do it again. If a child still doesn't hear the number of claps let her count the other children's names out loud. This experience can be used at the beginning of the school year to help children learn each other's names. Many children are shy and won't say their names clearly to a group. While we're still learning the names, I will stand behind each child and say it with him.

ME

VARIATION
Instead of clapping we could move different body parts the exact amount of times.

CATEGORIZING
We will now group ourselves according to how many syllables we have in our names. Let's say and clap each name.

> All ones, over here
> All twos, over there and
> All threes, over here.

How many children in the set of

ones? . . . . . twos? . . . . . threes? . . . . .

Possibly have cards with the numerals written on them placed in different areas. Children can recognize the number of syllables in their names and move toward their spot.

All children in the three set, say your
name nice and loud. Good! Say it louder!
Now together. Everyone in group three, say
your name nice and loud at the same time.
Ready! . . . Begin! . . . . Now the rest of the
children can be our orchestra. Clap three times, and
hold for a second . . . and again . . . Let's try it
together.

**At the beginning, the teacher can verbalize
1-2-3-hold to help keep everyone together.**

Group three, you will now do
"The Dance of Your Name."
Do one movement for each syllable, and freeze after
the last syllable. The orchestra will keep rhythm for you
by clapping. You may move any body part.

When you freeze be aware of the beautiful sculptures
you are making. Each one will be different.
Everyone has a different name.
Everyone is different.
So everyone's dance will be unique.

LIN

**This is repeated for each set of children for
two syllables, and one syllable, and possibly
for four, as in Elizabeth.**

**Kindergarteners may develop this name
experience over a few weeks. Fifth graders
could do it in a day.**

DA

39

The child for the day may teach her name dance to the rest of the class. Everyone is now doing the same dance. It is (Cynthia's) dance.

To help overcome self-consciousness, have a general warm up with everyone doing her name at the same time.

Cheers

FOR OLDER OR MORE EXPERIENCED GROUPS
Divide yourselves into groups of four. Each group will develop a dance or cheer by having each person create a movement to each syllable of his name, and then teach it to the others in your group.

Your group will then decide on the order and perform your dance or cheer for the entire class, saying the names along with the movements. Everyone in the group will perform all the names.

IN PARTNERS
Dance both first names as one. Such as (Anna-Maria, Sylvia-Joe). The rhythm of your names will be your music. Experiment with your movements, saying your names over and over again.

You might want to explore some locomotor movements such as hops, jumps, skips or leaps to create patterns for your name dances.

NAME
GAMES

Children love to hear their names. It makes them feel recognized, important and good about themselves. It also provides opportunities to recognize and support each other. I often use name games as a first experience to get to know each other or at the end of a lesson for a closing experience.

INTRODUCTIONS

Walk around the room and pretend to place your name in someone else's hand, while saying it out loud. Be aware of all the different ways each individual makes contact.

Add a positive quality to your name (something you like about yourself). Repeat this introduction to as many individuals as possible as you walk through the room. Example: "Hello, I'm Harlene and I'm very loving."

CIRCLE SWAY

Everyone in a circle, on your knees shoulder to shoulder. One person may stand in the middle. Very slowly and together, the circle group sway back from knees and forward, back and forth. As you come forward softly chant the name of the person standing in the middle. It is a unique experience for all.

Try it with no one in the middle, saying mmmmmmmmmmmmmmm and ahhhhhhhhhhhhh.

THE NAME SCREAM

This experience is helpful in freeing children to project their voices.

Walk around the room using the entire space, whispering your name to yourself. Say your name louder, and continue to let your body go with its rhythm. Let your whole body move. Arms, head, legs, trunk, shoulders, whatever it wants to do.

Say your name louder and exaggerate the movement. It is completely yours. It goes to the rhythm of your name.

Build this up until you are screaming your name as loud as you can, while running through the space with head, chest, and arms thrown open. Do it again . . . . Louder!

Now, without any sound at all, let your body scream your name as you move through the space. How can your body scream your name?

This may be helpful for children who scream at inappropriate times.

How about your address? Can you say that in rhythm? In movement? Is there a rhythm to what you are saying? Do you give more force to certain words?

Pick any phrase and experiment with it. Add small gestures, and then exaggerate them. Take these movements through space as you say your phrase or address.

To get childen to move rhythmically with awareness of counting, experiment with experience, Moving to Number Four, p. 31. Remind students about moving throughout the entire space freely without bumping into anyone else. This may need some practice by itself. See Moving Through Space Constructively, p. 27.

Expect a great deal of laughing especially in older groups, including adults. This is caused by embarrassment as well as fun. It subsides as participants begin to feel more comfortable with movement.

As children lose their shyness, they may be willing to perform their dances individually. While each child does his dance, the rest of the class supports him. They form a circle around the dancer, joining in on the chanting of the performer's name.

NAME WITH GESTURE

This is often an enjoyable way to begin a movement workshop for both children and adults.

Everyone may stand in a circle. First person, say your name along with a spontaneous gesture of how you are feeling at this very moment. The next person, repeat that name and gesture adding your own name with gesture. The third person, repeat the first two names and gestures, and add your own.

This continues until the last person around the circle can repeat all the names with the gestures and adds her own.

The entire group can now repeat this together saying each person's name with the gesture.

I have done this name experience with as many as twenty adults, and as few as four with five and six year olds. It is also good for memory and sequencing.

VARIATION I
Same as above except that entire group repeats the name with gesture, adding one more as each person gets his turn. This is much easier for small children.

VARIATION II
This variation takes much less time, and is a dramatic ice breaker. As each person takes a turn, the entire group immediately mirrors back the person's gesture and name. There is often laughter as each person reveals how he feels at that moment.

Extend this by breaking the circle formation, slightly altering your movement and using lots of space. Keep the theme of your gesture, letting it evolve by using different directions, levels and moving into as much space as possible.

We can call this "The Dance of Introduction."

SOME HINTS
Don't try to think of your gesture in advance. Do whatever comes naturally during your turn. *Sometimes a person will not be able to think of what to do and make a gesture of "I don't know." Use that as the gesture.*

GROUP NAME REINFORCEMENT

One person, stand in the middle of the circle. Those of you making the circle bend low with your arms extended to the back. Slowly rise, bringing your arms forward and up while moving towards the center of the circle. At the same time say the name of the person in the middle, letting your voices build louder and stronger as you reach the person in the center.

All of you who wish to, will have a chance in the center. It is a very powerful experience.

YOUR NAME
AND ANIMAL YOU LIKE

Say your name and an animal you like or relate to.
Take a few moments to be that animal.

"I am Karen the fish."

MOVE TO YOUR QUALITIES

Sit in groups of ten. Take turns saying your name accompanied by an adjective with the same first letter. For example, "I'm Terry the Terror", "I'm Barbara the Beautiful", "I'm Angry Angie", "I'm Laughing Lou".

Add an appropriate gesture that shows the feeling of the descriptive words.

You may expand this gesture to a whole body movement/dance using the entire available space.

VARIATION
Say your name and what you would like to have, what you would like to be or something in nature. Give yourself a title such as Prince Lawrence or Countess Maria.

LANGUAGE

Creative movement provides a basis in the body for making letters and words more meaningful. The more children experience in life, the richer becomes their receptive and expressive language. By responding to their sensory input, children learn.

RIGHT AND LEFT

Everyone sit on the floor, legs stretched out in front of you. With both hands, vigorously slap your right leg up and down, front and back. Not too hard. Don't hurt yourselves. Do this for one minute. Sit quietly and feel the difference between both legs. How does the right leg feel? How does the left leg feel?

Raise your right hand . . . Wave it . . . Touch your right foot . . . Crawl the fingers of your right hand up your right leg and touch your right ear.
　Stamp your right foot and slap your right side.
　　Fall to the floor on your right side . . . What parts of your body are touching the floor?
　　　Move your right shoulder up and down.
　　　　Wink your right eye.
　　　　　Touch your right ear to your right shoulder.

YOU MAKE UP SOME MORE!

　Your right elbow to your right ____?____ .
　　Your right hand to your left ____?____ .
　　　Right wrist to left ____?____ .
　　　　Shake your right ____?____ .

WHAT ELSE CAN YOU DO?

　Skip to the right,
　　jump to the left,
　tip toe to the right,
　　slide to the left,
　run to the right,
　　hop to the left,
　point to the right,
　　punch to the left,
　fall to the right.

　　MARCHING
Signal . . . right turn . . . .
left turn . . . **and so on.**

51

WITH PARTNERS
Shake someone's right hand. Why are you using opposite hands? Figure it out.

Touch your right foot to someone else's right foot . . . Your right hip to someone else's right hip. Your right shoulder to someone else's right _____ .

Keep it going with suggestions coming from the participants. It gets to be a lot of fun.

DANCING IT
Choose a body part on your right side. Let it lead you around the room in a dance. Let the rest of your body follow it as it dips, turns and moves through space.

Find a partner. Decide what parts of your body will be stuck together . . . two right arms . . . two left shoulders . . . two right legs. etc.

Find all the possible ways you can move in this position with your partner. Make it a dance.

SELF MASSAGE

Self slapping can be extended to the entire body for an invigorating self massage.

You can also work with a partner, one partner standing and hanging over the other. The other may go up and down the back, legs, and arms using the slapping technique. Get feedback from your partner if slapping is too hard or not hard enough. It's also fun to do this with two partners working on one person.

THE GOLDEN GOOSE

Close your eyes and walk around the room slowly. Use different levels and create a slow motion dance forming different sculptures. When you touch another person, you are stuck and can no longer move.

After a few minutes everyone should be attached in some way resulting in a sometimes humorous sculpture.

Open your eyes and verbalize what body parts are touching.

Describe the scene.
For example: "Ann, your right hand is stuck to Eric's right knee." "Carolyn, your right ear is stuck to Brian's left shoulder" . . . and so on. This is based on the fairy tale, THE GOLDEN GOOSE.

STRAIGHT AND ROUND

STRAIGHT
Let's experiment with straight. Can you straighten your hands?
Your arms? Your whole body?

Create a straight sculpture! Everything
is straight. Good! Make a different
one. Yes! Now change it again.
Everyone has a different shape.
And they are all straight. Feel
the straightness everywhere . . . .
toes . . . back . . . neck.

Create a straight dance by changing
positions . . . Take a step into
space each time you change
your shape. Connect with
someone who is near you,
still creating your straight
dance. Move around the
room! Now connect
with someone else.

Can you be straight
and high? Can you be
straight and on a low
level? Yes, that's great!

Continue your straight
dance and be on any
level you wish.

*Since letters, numbers and
shapes have round and
straight pathways, I always
begin with the concept of
straight and round before
introducing them.*

ROUNDNESS

Now let's feel round. Can you make your fingers and hands round . . .
Now your arms . . . nice and round. How about your back? Your toes!

Everything nice and soft and round. Make a beautiful round
shape! Good! Now another one! A different one. Everyone
making a different round shape, because everyone is different.

Can you make a round shape on the floor? On a
low level? Change it! How about a round shape
from a sitting position! Keep changing it. Make
as many different round shapes as you can.

Find two partners and be a group of three.
All connected and round. They are
beautiful! Change the shape.
Change it again!

Move in round shapes
around each other. An
ongoing dance of round
shapes with your partners
. . . keep changing your
shapes . . . and keep all
parts of your body
round and soft.

See Space Flow, p. 23.

PATTERNING LETTERS

Using yarn or rope, shape the letter 'B' on the floor large enough for an entire class to stand around.

Who knows what letter this is? . . . . 'B'. . . . . Very good! Who would like to show me the part of the 'B' that is round? Good! Now show me the part that is straight . . . . Yes!

We will move around the 'B', straightening our bodies on the straight part and rounding our bodies on the round part of the 'B'.

If this is too difficult for some children, begin by creating a simple free form shape with one round section and one straight section for the children to follow.

What does the letter 'B' sound like? Yes, very good! What words do you know that begin with the sound of 'B'?

Try to elicit moving words, or words easy to act out, such as ball, big, bounce, or balloon. Put two of the 'B' words together such as bouncing ball . . . . big bear . . . . or beautiful balloon.

Everyone go in the same direction. Be the bouncing ball as you move around the 'B'.

Also say its sound as in b . . . . b . . . . . . b . . . . . Bouncing ball. Keep repeating as you move around the 'B' as a bouncing ball.

Most of the time I look in the dictionary to find action words for each letter. They don't have to make sense. They could be funny, as in flying fish or happy hippo. See p. 58 for some ideas.

We are learning through the senses by verbalizing, hearing, seeing, and feeling the letters through movement.

While letter 'B' is on the floor, you may develop other concepts such as:

Everyone may stand around the letter patterned on the floor. Put one foot inside the 'B'. Take your foot out. Put two hands and one foot inside. How many body parts do you have inside? Three! Good!

Now put four body parts in. Good! (Talisha) has two hands, one foot and one elbow in. (William) has one head, one arm and two feet in.

Continue with different numbers of body parts.

Place your fingers on the 'B'. Take your fingers off. Walk around the letter 'B'. Skip . . . . March . . . . Hop . . . . Jump . . . . Slide.

These experiences can also be done with shapes, numbers, a clock, maps of cities and countries or any other outline of things we are learning about. See Using Yarn, p. 129, and the illustration on p. 61.

MORE ALPHABET WORDS FOR MOVEMENT

A   Angry Alligator

B   Bouncing Ball

C   Crawling Cat

D   Dancing Dolls

E   Easy Eggs

F   Flying Fingers — Flying Feet

G   Go Go Go
(marching and punching)

H   Hopping High

I   I I I (pointing proudly to self)

J   Jumping Jacks

K   k-k-k-k-k-Kick

L   Leaping Long

M   Marching Merrily

N   No No No (stamping and shaking head)

K K K K KICK

O   Oh Oh Open

P   Punching Pillows

Q   Quickly and Quietly

R   Running Races

S   Sliding Slowly

T   Tip Toe Tip Toe

U   Under and Up

V   Vibrating Vigorously

W   Winding Winds

X   x-x-x (Jumping,
crisscrossing arms and legs)

Y   Yes Yes Yes Yes Yes Yes (in rhythm)

Z   ZigZagging

GO GO GO

58

QU . . . . QUIET

FLYING FINGERS FLYING FEET

SOME TASTE SOUNDS

A	Apple	J	Jello	R	Radish
B	Banana	K	Ketchup	S	Salt
C	Cookie	L	Lollipop	T	Turnip
D	Doughnut	M	Milk	V	Vinegar
E	Egg	N	Nuts	W	Watermelon
F	Fish	O	Olives	Y	Yogurt
G	Greens	P	Peas	Z	Zucchini
H	Honey	Q	Quiche		
I	Ice cream				

VARIATIONS WITH PATTERNING

MUSICAL STAFF
Pattern a musical staff.
Jump from one space or line to another, creating words. **See p. 147.**

FREE FORM SHAPES
**Create free-form shapes making straight and round patterns throughout the room.
See Using Yarn, p. 129.**
Follow the patterns, and let your body respond round or straight.

HOPSCOTCH
Make a hopscotch pattern using tape. Place it near the door so that children will hopscotch into the room.

SITTING AROUND LETTER
Students may sit around the yarn-shaped letter while continuing more formal parts of the lesson, such as finding where the letter 'B' or 'b' is printed around the room, or looking for picture words with that sound.

GROUP LETTER
With a large group, students can pick up the yarn, still keeping the shape of the letter.
Change the letter 'B' to 'D'. Good! Now make it an 'R'. See who has to move. Yes, very good!

This takes a great deal of cooperation.

INDIVIDUAL ROPES
Provide individual ropes for children so that they form their own letters to move with. The yarn can easily and quickly be put down and picked up again.

ALTERNATIVES TO YARN

MASKING TAPE
Masking tape is more permanent and will stay in place approximately a month. Children will begin to be aware of letter shape as a special space to play within. Sometimes they will even use its boundaries as a track for a toy car.

MUSICAL CHAIRS
Place the chairs in the formation of a letter. Children march around saying the sound of the letter. At a signal all will sit, including teacher, which leaves one less chair. The child left standing has the chance to move around by himself, using any locomotor movement. All will participate by saying the sound. No one wins or loses.

CHALK
Chalk is good for writing on pavement outdoors.

How many steps does
it take to go around
this square?
See Measuring Space, p. 28.

SKY WRITING

Print a large 'B' on the chalkboard.

Everyone face toward the 'B' . . . Pretend that you put some chalk on your finger. Now point your finger high in the air in front of you. Draw a straight line down. Go back to the top of the line, then around and around to the bottom of the line.

What other body part can you draw with? Your foot? Good! Put some chalk on your foot. You show us and we'll follow. Good! Everyone did it. What other body part?

Elbow . . . hip . . . shoulder . . . nose . . . knee . . . eye . . . teeth . . . belly . . . tongue . . . whole body.

Use any body part the children name.

Draw the largest 'B' you can with your arm. Draw the smallest 'B' you can with your finger.

Emphasize going from left to right, and from top to bottom.

Let it flow.

In a continuous dance of changing body parts, flow through the space writing your letter in the air.

With a partner, draw a letter in the air with someone else's body part. Move your partner through space to extend the letter.

Skywriting is especially good for reversals, such as 'b' and 'd'. I usually just work with the 'b', moving the round part to the right to limit confusion.

Touch the body part used for skywriting. **This helps focus and reinforces concentration.**

Be a clock. Use your arms to point to what time it is. For example: one arm straight up, and the other pointing down for six o'clock.

Draw the letter on your partner's back. Have her guess what you wrote.

This activity can also be done with numbers and shapes.

THE LETTER DANCE

Choose the first letter of your name. Imagine it patterned on the floor.

Now imagine your whole body as a pencil. Bend . . . Turn . . . . Twist . . . . Swoop . . . . Curve . . . . as do the letters of your name, following the same pattern on the floor.

Divide the class in half.

Half the class may sit on the sides of the room. You will be the audience. The rest, find a space in the room that is not too close to each other, walls, or furniture. Use the entire space.

You are the dancers. Dancers are all going to create their own letter using as much of the entire space as possible. Imagine how your letter will begin and position or sculpture yourself accordingly.

Now using your whole body and all the available space, write the first letter of your name. Use all the up, down, and swirly movements you imagine it to have. When you are finished, pause in a finished position. Have a sense of the beginning and ending of your letter.

Repeat this three times.

Dancers and audience change places.

Use the dance form to spell out your entire first name. Begin and end each letter separately. Each letter can begin from a different place in the room. You need not be limited to printing (or writing) in a straight line.

As a variation suggest moving from one letter to the next in a continuous flow.

These alphabet exercises can also be used for spelling words, cursive writing, blends, numerals or shapes.

Scribbling

FOR PRESCHOOL CHILDREN
Use your whole body as if it were a crayon. You are going to use the entire space as if it were a drawing paper. I want you to scribble all over the paper. Make little scribbles and big scribbles. Use the whole space. Use a little space.

A REVIEW LETTER GAME

Freeze in the shape of letter 'T'. Now tiptoe saying the sound of 'T'. Freeze as a 'T'. Now touch someone . . . . freeze as a 'T'. Now be a Tiger . . . . freeze as a 'T'.

Move freely around the room. When I say "freeze", form the letter 'A'. Next time find a different way.

LETTER SCULPTING

Form the letter 'B' with your body. Wonderful! Look at all the different ways you can make a 'B'.

FOR VERY YOUNG CHILDREN
If one or two children succeed in forming the letter, have the whole class do it with them. Eventually as you go through the other letters of the alphabet more children will find their own ways.

Make the letter 'B' from a lying down position . . . A sitting position . . . . A standing position.

Make the letter 'B' with a partner . . . Now in small groups of three or four . . . . . And now the entire class.

CREATE A GROUP LETTER SCULPTURE
Choose someone's name, i.e. "Beth".

First person, shape a 'B' with your body.

Second person, attach to 'B' while shaping an 'E'.

Third person, attach to one or both partners, and shape a 'T'.

Last person, attach to any of the letters from any direction and shape an 'H'.
See Levels, p. 102.

MORE SCULPTING

Use this sculpting technique for numbers, shapes, and spelling.

FOR OLDER CHILDREN
While standing, position yourselves so that the whole group is shaping a letter. Begin with an easy letter, and continue to do more difficult ones. Try to do this without talking.

Ending with the letter 'O' brings everyone together again, ready for a new adventure or transition to another lesson. This experience is also good for fostering group cooperation and problem solving.

Children enjoy helping with straightening or rounding each other's bodies for the different letters.

FEELING SHAPES

Close your eyes and listen to your breathing.

Very gently touch your face. Feel your cheekbones,
  outlines of your nose,
    eyes,
      mouth,
        and ears.

Feel your hair . . . . . examine your hair line. Become aware of the different textures of your face and hair. What parts are soft,
                    hard . . . ,
                  rough . . . ,
                smooth . . . ,
                  cold . . . ,
                  warm . . . ,
                    straight, round?
                      Feel all the shapes!

WITH PARTNERS
With eyes closed, take turns exploring each other's face and head. Be aware of how the shapes are different. Be totally nonverbal. Be very gentle.

When finished, open your eyes, and verbally share with your partner how you felt exploring each other's face.

How did it feel to have your own face explored?

Share with the entire group how it felt to discover your own face in this way.

Share any other feelings you might have experienced.

Some children may not be able to keep their eyes closed. Let them continue with their eyes open.

'Z'
Sound

ALPHABET SOUNDS

Create a hand or arm gesture or small body movement for each sound of the alphabet.

These hand gestures can later be extended to the entire body, and to movement throughout the general space. Make up your own gestures with the class.

Everyone sit in a circle. Say the 'Z' sound over and over again allowing your body to react naturally to the sound. Be aware of the movement that your body is making to the sound, and let it repeat itself over and over.

Eventually a few different movements will emerge from the constant chanting of the sound.

Exaggerate the movement so it is a definite and repeatable gesture.

'D'
Sound

DEVELOP A DANCE
String a few of these movements together while saying their sounds. Try using all the vowels, a-e-i-o-u, or the letters in someone's name. Create a vowel dance with a partner. Experiment and have fun.

Sharon Brill created the idea for gestures for alphabet sounds when doing her student teaching with me in the kindergarten classroom. She was then a dance education student at Temple University. The final array of gestures written here came from many sources including the children, teachers and participants in workshops.

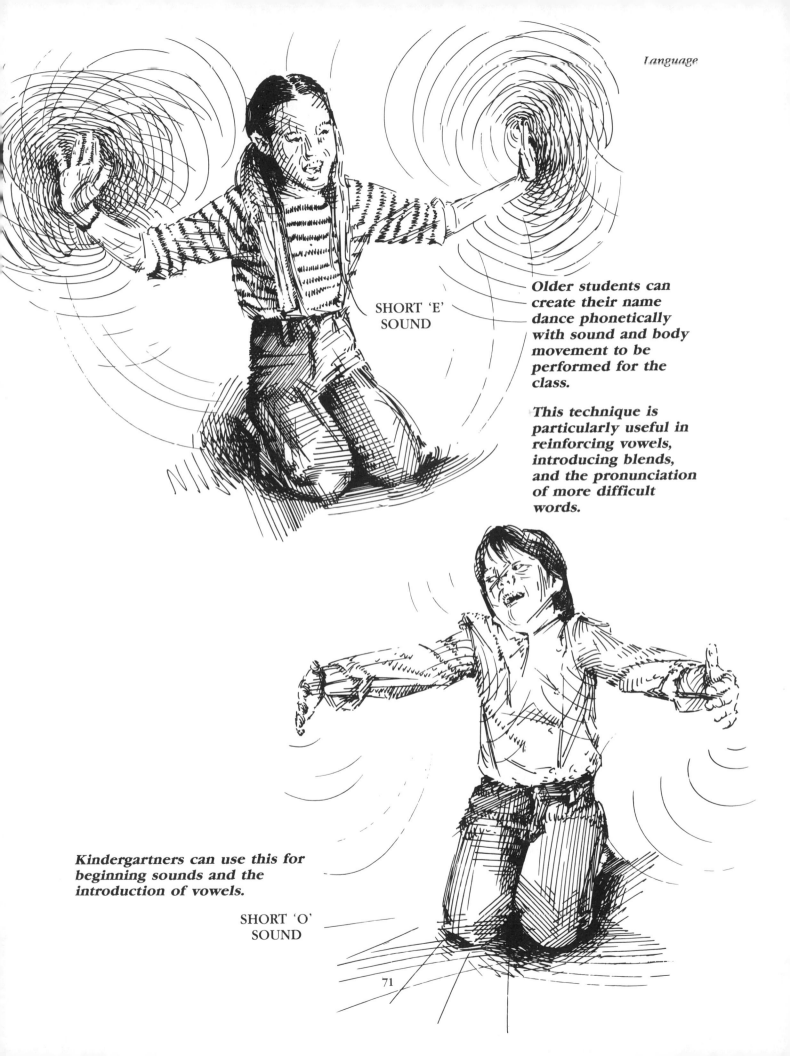

SHORT 'E'
SOUND

Older students can create their name dance phonetically with sound and body movement to be performed for the class.

This technique is particularly useful in reinforcing vowels, introducing blends, and the pronunciation of more difficult words.

Kindergartners can use this for beginning sounds and the introduction of vowels.

SHORT 'O'
SOUND

'V' SOUND

SUGGESTIONS FOR GESTURES OF LETTER SOUNDS

Ă	"I don't care", wave of the hand
Ā	Thumbs up, (The Fonze)
B	B o u n c i n g
C	Cutting
D	Finger on mouth (Dopey, as in "The Seven Dwarfs")
Ĕ	Pushing motion
Ē	Fingers wiggling straight out in front, (a scary motion)
F	Arms flying
G	Locomotor fists
H	Hand sweeps across brow as in "hot"

Ĭ	Pointing disgustingly
Ī	Pointing to yourself proudly
J	Arms jumping rope
K	Finger under nose as if sneezing
L	Licking a lollypop, (taffy)
M	Mmmmmmmmmmmm, rubbing tummy as if eating something good
N	Shaking head "no"
Ŏ	Opening arms slowly with pleasure
Ō	Hands open on both sides of mouth as if exclaiming "Oh"!
P	Puffing into fists. (feel the wind)

'K' SOUND

'I'
SOUND

QU	Hands opening and closing as if a duck quacking
R	Quickly weaving your hand away from your body
S	Undulating arm as if a snake
T	Arm raised, elbow resting in other hand, moving back and forth as in tictoc, tictoc
Ŭ	Arms struggling up
Ū	Pointing at others saying you-you-you

V   Whole body vibrating

W   Arms waving in the wind

X   A sawing movement of one hand across the other arm

Y   Head nodding "yes"

Z   Hand with fingers pinched together moving fast in all directions like a bee.

'G' SOUND

PERIOD
DANCE

PUNCTUATION MARKS

Shape the punctuation marks with your body. Draw them in the air with different body parts. Pattern them on the floor. Now create a movement that says "Period", and another that shows a question. What kind of movement or series of movements would show a comma? How about an exclamation mark?

Now expand this movement into a series of movements that could be a dance.

Play a guessing game. Someone acts out one of the punctuation marks or dances it, and the rest of the class may guess what it is.

Play with a sentence such as "I am going away." *Have the students act out the different punctuation marks. Each time read the sentence with the emphasis on a different word, and hear how the meaning changes.*

Create other sentences you can do that with.

As a short story is read, students can act out the punctuation marks at the appropriate times.

COMMA
DANCE

ALPHABET GAMES

Place the lower case letters (on cards) around the floor. Children will hold the capital letters in their hands. The leader calls a letter. The child with that letter will move to its matching one on the floor. The movement will be appropriate to the letter's sound. All students will say its sound as the child is moving. See Alphabet Sounds, pgs. 70-73.

B	S	E	L	T
D	V	H	U	O
G	X	K	W	Y
J	Z	N	A	R
C	F	I	M	P

EXCLAMATION DANCE

Create a grid on the floor. Use tape, chalk, or put it on a large paper. Give the following directions:

Jump to letter 'A'.

Hop to the first letter of your name.

Leap to each letter of your name.

Place your hand on 'Z', your right foot on 'H' and your left foot on 'P'.

Throw a bean bag on 'W'.

Bounce a ball four times on 'B'.

Create your own directions.

Make a grid with numbers, shapes, pictures, or anything else you can think of.

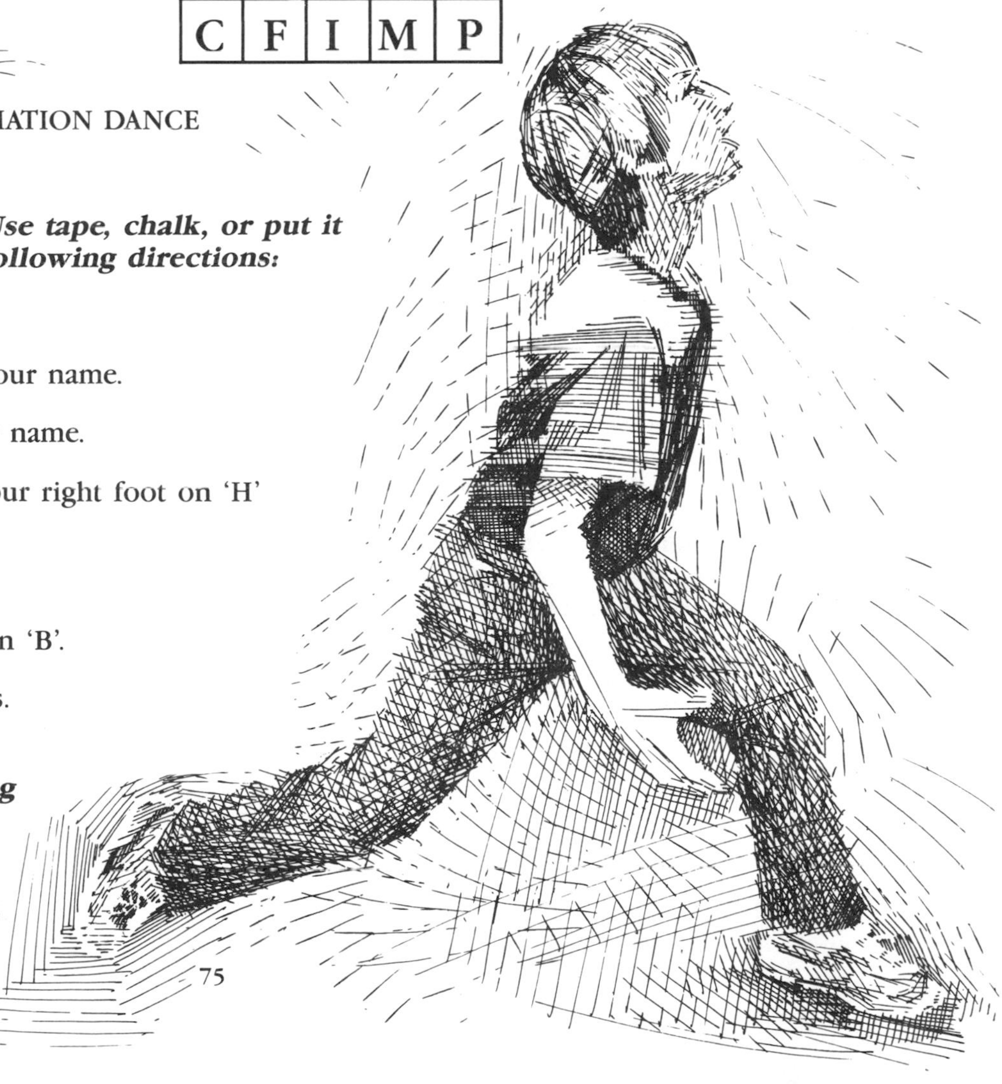

A QUESTION DANCE

75

WORDS WORDS WORDS

Warm-up with a series of words.

Begin by sitting quietly and listening to your breathing. Start to stretch your face in all possible ways. Twist and stretch all the muscles . . . Your mouth, nose, forehead . . . Now begin to stretch your spine, bringing yourself to a standing position. Rise slowly, twisting and stretching your whole body . . . Shake! . . . . Shake your whole body . . . Freeze! . . . . Melt . . . . Very slowly melt to the floor . . . . Tighten up into a ball . . . Relax . . . . Roll . . . Roll, just keep rolling. Roll over each other when you meet. Do it carefully and freeze! Stand quickly! . . . Skip . . . Skip higher and higher . . . . . Freeze! Twitch . . . Keep twitching . . . . Freeze! Collapse! Curl into a very tight ball and release. Stretch out again and start to curl tightly and release. Crawl! Rise in slow motion. Walk in slow motion. Talk in slow motion, saying anything . . . . your name, address, anything. Slowly connect with others in slow motion. Pull each other in slow motion and freeze. Relax . . . .

Change the words. String them together so that you alternate moving in place with movements that will take you through space.

Use lying down movements and standing movements. Make it possible to go from one to the other.

Find more words in the dictionary you would like to use.

CHOREOGRAPHY WITH WORDS

SWING AND SWAY
Standing in place, let your body experience a gentle sway. That's good! Now let the sway get larger . . . . Let your arms get into it and make it larger! . . . . Let the sway develop into a swing. Bend from the waist . . . . Make it big . . . . . Swing up and down, forward and backward, side to side. Use your whole body . . . Let the momentum of your body take you through the room. Yes, that's wonderful!

Now let's make it smaller . . . . Bring the swing down . . . . Slower, gently . . . . Back to a small sway. Feel the sway inside your body. Your whole body feels the sway . . . . . Sway very slightly in place until you are not moving at all . . . Relax . . . . .

This can also be used as an experience in developing range of movement from small to large, from standing in place to using the entire space, or from body parts to whole body.

SCOOP
REACH
RUN
TILT

Using just these four words, create your own dance. Say these words in order, over and over again.

Choose your own words and create your own combinations for a dance.

WORDS WITH A THEME

Write as many one word associations as you can think of on a theme such as water. These might include ocean, waves, lake, ducks, boats, river, rushing, smooth, rough, brook, pool, fountain, splashing, puddle, rain, snow, ice, frozen, melting.

Use a piece of music which expresses the feelings of the various water words stated, such as THE THIEVING MAGPIE.

Ask the group to "be the waves, . . . be the ocean", and so forth, feeling it in their bodies as they move throughout the room. Make sure your voice conveys the feelings associated with the words. With young children you may want to experience each word separately for a while. For example, "Let's find all the movements we can create for waves . . . . rain" . . . etc.

OTHER THEMES

SPRING
Flowers, birth, newness, opening, love, birds, laughing

FLAMES
Flying, hurrying, whipping, rising, spurting

CLOUDS
Flowing, drifting, tossing, falling, bursting, soft, gentle

DESCRIBE YOURSELF

Descriptions could change with each group. There are no "correct" descriptions, only what individuals are feeling at that moment.

VERBS AND ADVERBS

Have verbs and adverbs printed on flash cards. (Have one list longer than the other so that the combinations can continually change.)

Two people will hold the cards and flash them to the group on the opposite side of the room. Individuals will move across the room in response to the combinations such as:

run quickly	walk slowly	slide smoothly
skip gaily	jump twitchingly	tiptoe quickly
angrily hop	sleepily wiggle	arrogantly tumble
quietly leap	hostilely turn	shyly roll

COMMUNICATION

Learning to work together in creative collaboration is based upon our ability to communicate wants, needs, feelings, and thoughts clearly and appropriately.

Sometimes, people give and receive mixed messages. We verbally say "yes" while our body language says "no". This can be confusing to the person we're talking to as well as to ourselves. By becoming aware of what we really want to communicate, our messages will become more direct, honest, and open. The responses we receive will be more truthful and appropriate to our needs.

Movement, the heart and soul of nonverbal communication, expands our awareness, heightens our sensitivity, and enhances our verbal skills.

GIVING GIFTS

Some soft lovely music is needed for this. I like to use Judy Collins singing SUZANNE.

Sit crosslegged or otherwise comfortably across from your partner. One partner will nonverbally give a gift to the other. You don't necessarily need to be thinking of something specific. Take the gift "from above", "pick it from the ground", "catch it in the air", or anything else you can think of. It might be a moonbeam, an article of clothing, a piece of jewelry, or a flower, etc. Give it with loving feelings. You may place the gift in your partner's hands, or around her shoulders, or just shower her with it. Your partner does not need to know what the gift is, but will have a feeling for it. The receiver may then take time with the receiving, luxuriating in the gift, and finally placing it somewhere, if appropriate. She then takes her turn in giving a gift to her partner. This goes back and forth. ***It can easily last five minutes or the length of time of the piece of music.***

Verbally share your
feelings and ideas
about what you
thought the
gifts were
and how
you felt
about
receiving
and
giving
them.

"Gifts" was another experience I enjoyed in Poldi Orlando's workshops, and giving was very much a part of Poldi.

BACK TO BACK

Find a partner and sit back-to-back. Close your eyes and silently contact your partner's back. Without moving, be aware of the physical sensation. What parts of your back are being contacted?

Now, gently and slowly, begin to move your backs, interacting with your partner as if in conversation. What is your partner's back like? How does it feel? Push back and forth. Who is more forceful? Who is more gentle?

One of you lean back as far as you can and relax for a moment.

Now, reverse. How does it feel to be leaned on and to support another? How does it feel to lean and be supported? Which do you prefer?

Find other ways you can move with your partner's back. Gradually bring your head, arms, and hands into this interaction. Let the movement flow into a dance. Add music, and let the dance happen for awhile . . . . Now, slowly let your backs say goodbye and slightly bend forward. Quietly absorb what you have just experienced. How does it feel to be separated? Turn around and take a few moments to verbally share your feelings about this experience.

In a standing position find all the ways you can dance with your partner in a back-to-back position. Begin to move throughout the space.

MIRRORING

Face a partner. One will be the leader, and the other will be the mirror. It is easier to begin with just hands. Then slowly add head, shoulders, torso, and legs. The mirror acts just like a mirror image of the partner. The leader should not make any sudden movements. When partners are feeling comfortable, they may slowly move through space. Use different levels of high and low.

Change roles. Try mirroring each other without anyone being a leader or follower. Just let it happen. Leadership may flow back and forth until you yourselves don't know who is leading or who is following. You are moving as one. This can become a very deep experience.

Music is optional. If music is used, it needs to be slow. Mirroring in silence creates another feeling.

VARIATIONS

OPPOSITES
This is the same idea as mirroring, but instead, do the opposite movement.

EXTENDING
Leader, create a short movement and then freeze. Mirror, extend or complete the leader's movement, and then add your own . . . . Leader, now extend the mirror's movement, and add your own. This can become a conversation going back and forth.

DELAYED
Leader, create a movement and then freeze . . . . . Mirror, first watch and then repeat it. Do this a few times before changing roles.

MIRRORING FOR AWARENESS
How would you like to see yourself? Get into your strength. Make strong movements. Watch your ''mirror'' and see the feedback. Get into your gentleness. Make soft movements. Watch the feedback in your mirror as you move. How close do you want to be to your partner? How much distance are you comfortable with? Leader decides, mirror will cooperate and tune into his own feelings of comfort with partner's needs.

MIRRORING THE ENERGY
Get into the feeling and energy flow of your partner. Follow your partner wherever she goes and stop when she stops. It is not an exact mirroring, but more like getting into the rhythms and shapes.

MAGNETS

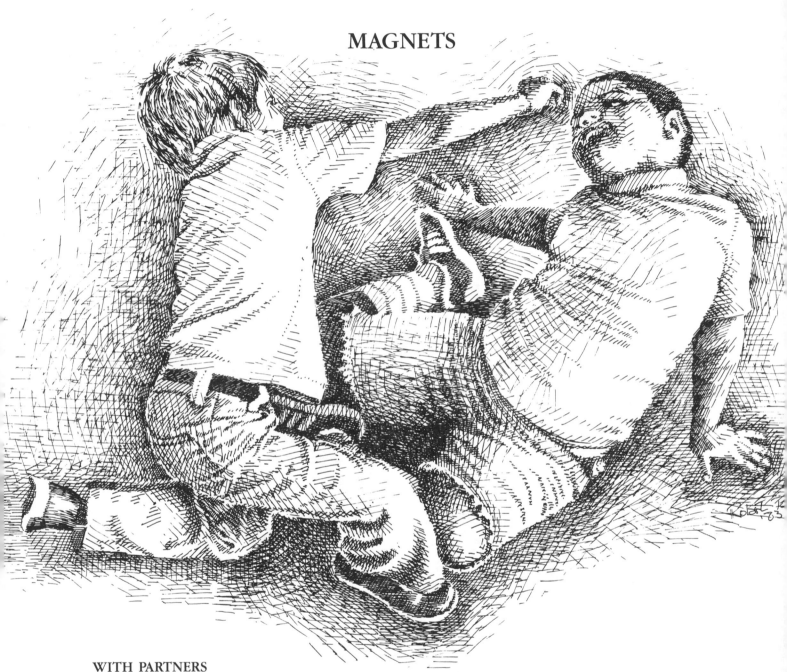

WITH PARTNERS

We will make believe partner "A's" hand is a magnet. Partner "B's" nose will be magnetized. As "A" moves his hand, "B" will respond accordingly, moving as if attracted by the magnet. Also, as much as possible, keep your feet planted in one spot on the floor. We want you to have to twist, bend, go up or down, possibly roll over, bend backwards, etc. as you follow the magnet. We want you to get into as many positions as you can create.   Change roles.

Sit down with your partner and share verbally with him how it felt to be the magnet and to be the one who is magnetized. Which did you like better? You might try doing this with different partners.

INDIVIDUAL MAGNETS

Everyone, sit down in your own space. Make believe one of your hands is a magnet and the rest of your body is magnetized. What happens when you bring the magnet to your knee? To your foot? Play with it, and see how that part of your body reacts. How about your head, your stomach, your other hand?

Create a dance in slow motion, moving your hand around one part of your body, stimulating it to move in different ways, and then working with another body part.

GROUP

Everybody bunch together, all facing the same direction. One person, face the group. With your magnet hand, indicate which way you want the group to move, and the group will respond as one. You will be like an orchestra leader with the group swaying left or right, up or down as indicated.

Give as many individuals as possible a chance to lead. It is a very unusual experience. It gives a feeling of tremendous power for the leader, produces togetherness in the group, and provides a learning experience about leader-group dynamics, as well as the physical phenomenon of magnetism.

CAUSE AND AFFECT

The "magnets" experience can also be done with the idea of "winds and leaves". In partners, one will be the wind and the other will be the leaf. The wind will use an arm to show the leaf which way it is blowing, and the leaf will respond. The wind can indicate direction:

> *fast or slow,*
> > *levels: high, medium, low,*
> > > *floating,*
> > > > *twirling.*

Wind . . . . . Allow your whole body to be the force that makes the leaf move. All of your body will push and move to show your power. Are you strong gusts which start and stop? Are you a gentle breeze with a constant even flow?

Leaves . . . . You are to move as your partner, the wind, directs you. Remember you are light and gentle, and the slightest force of the wind will create a movement in you.

COMMUNICATION WITH HANDS

Sit on the floor facing your partner. Touch each other's hands. Explore each other's hands simultaneously. Be aware of the messages you are giving and receiving. Are your partner's hands strong? Gentle? Firm? Loose? Quick? Slow? Rough? Light? Energized? Soft?

Stop and verbally share experiences, giving your partner feedback.

Try it again. This time respond to my words. Let your hands express happiness . . . shyness . . . compassion . . . love . . . sadness . . . anger . . . playfulness . . .

Dance together with your hands; let them whisper to each other, walk together . . . Skip . . . Run or move in slow motion . . . as if you are in water.

What are you feeling right now? Express that feeling to your partner with your hands. Now relax your hands in your own laps and verbally share the experience with your partner. Find out if your partner received the nonverbal message of how you felt.

Conversations With Whole Body

IN PARTNERS:

First partner, make a large movement statement. Second partner, respond with a movement using the entire body. Respond back and forth in conversation making statements or questions and answering. Use the entire body. Move through the space if necessary to make your movement point. An entire story or situation can be spontaneously created. When you're finished, verbally share the experience with your partner.

Try this with three or more partners. You may be able to write a short play from the different movement scenes. It is not necessary to have specific meaning.

COMMUNICATION DANCE

WITH ARMS
      LEGS
         HEAD
           TORSO

Arrange yourselves into groups of six. We are going to do an arm dance. Nobody will be leading, no one will follow. Create your own movements, yet still be aware of everyone else's movements. Interact cooperatively, arms only, and develop your own dance together. Everyone, be aware of each other in your group while you maintain your uniqueness.

Change groups. Work with those you haven't worked with yet. Do a head dance. Find all the possible ways you can move your head, including those in relationship to each other.

With each different body part, change groups, so that you get a chance to work with as many different people as possible. Changing partners stimulates different types of movement. It is also a way to get to know everyone better.

Now try this with a leg dance. Do you want to keep standing or would you like to lie down and bring your legs up in the air? In any way you would like, create a leg dance. How will they relate to the other legs you will come in contact with?

How about a torso dance? No other part of your body is moving. Just your torso. How will your torso create a dance? How will it dance with the other torsos in your group?

Try this with partners,
and in smaller groups
of three or four.

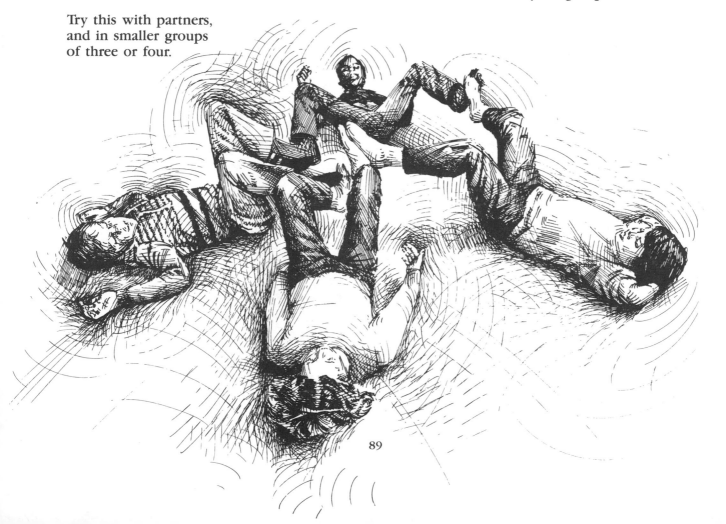

NO TOUCH FIGHTING

In an environment of safety, spontaneity, and support, many exciting movement happenings may evolve. A lot of aggression can be discharged safely while children come to understand the consequences of fighting, both as giver and receiver.

A group of fourth graders began their movement lesson saying their names in syllables using a strong punch movement. This evolved into an improvisation on fighting. We then had to set down some rules for ourselves.

We cannot touch anyone else.

All our movements will be in slow motion.

Take the time to respond to the punch and how different parts of the body should react to the energy coming toward you.

Begin by working with partners and expand to small group "brawls". Let the drama unfold.

Reinforce that there is no body contact, and the actions are in slow motion.

MOVEMENT GAMES AND WARM UPS

Movement games and warm-ups can bring individuals together as a group in a fun and easy way. They can be used to warm up the body, lessen self-consciousness, and help the children to enjoy moving and creating with each other.

HANDS AND OTHER BODY PARTS

Everyone may come into a circle and sit down. **Use rhythmic music.** Can you move your hands like this? Good! Someone show us a different way we can move our hands . . . . Everyone do it . . . . Someone show us a different way . . . . Very good!

You can continue like this until everyone has a turn to change the movement. Everyone together in a circle doing the same thing is a good way to bring a group together and to get their attention before another lesson.

Let's do the same with the head. How many different ways can we find to move the head? How about shoulders? . . .

        Hips? . . .

        Legs? . . .

What other body parts can we move? How many different ways can we move them?

TOTAL GROUP STRETCH

Everyone, stand in a circle. Each person will take his turn to stretch out a different body part in a different way.

By the time everyone gets a turn each person should have all parts of his body stretched out and warmed up.

VARIATION
Stand in a circle. One person go into the middle and respond to the music in your own way. Everyone else do the same movement . . . . Now the person in the middle may stand in front of someone. That person may replace the individual in the center. She will change the movement and the group will follow. Continue until all have had a chance in the middle.

Everyone, continue the old movement until the next person changes it. There are no pauses between changes. This will keep the flow going.

BODY PARTS

I use this one with young children to get the class's attention.

Put your hands on your head, shoulders, knees, elbows, nose, etc.

Usually by the third body part everyone is together and focusing on the leader. To expand body awareness I will also use unfamiliar body parts such as nostril, navel, or earlobes.

RUBBER BANDS

In partners, hold hands or wrists. Stretch each other in all directions as if you were made of elastic. Have fun creating many different shapes and give each other a good stretch. Move as one piece of wire.

Try the same with everyone holding hands in a circle; pulling, twisting, stretching in slow motion.

MAGIC BLOB

With everyone sitting in a circle, I begin by making believe I have something in my hand. It could be something like clay or silly putty. I may do one or two different things with it such as: stretch it long, roll it, knead it, bounce it, throw it up in the air, chew it (yuk!), make a pizza. Then I pass it to the next person, and she does something different. This is a great quieting game and good for creative thinking.

BODY PHONE

Everyone, stand in a circle. Do not hold hands. Close your eyes. A chosen person will stand in front of one of the people in the circle and move him in a simple way, such as moving his body from the waist, down and up again. The person who was moved then opens his eyes and repeats the same movement to the person next to him. This goes around until everyone is moved.

Was the last person moved in the same way as the original? Where did it change? How did it change?

There will be a great deal of laughing as this is done. The people who still have eyes closed will start to wonder what's happening. Ask how it felt while they had their eyes closed. This is good for communication skills. Discuss how a story can become changed as it is told from person to person. The ability to reproduce a movement that you've experienced can develop your body awareness.

FOLLOW THE LEADER

Through nonverbal directions the leader can get her partner to walk, run, or jump in different directions, roll, get up, stop, etc. This could be a lot of fun. Make sure the follower gets a turn at being the leader.

THE TRIANGLE

In groups of three, everyone face the same way, standing in the formation of a triangle. The person in front may create any movement she feels in response to the music. The two partners in back will follow. At the signal you will all face a different direction putting another person from your triangle in the lead. She will change the movement with her partners following her. We will do this once again for your third person.

This can also be done in groups of four in diamond formation.

EXAGGERATE THE MOVEMENT

Get into small groups of six to ten. One person may begin a small movement and the whole group will follow. Allow that movement to get larger and larger until it is exaggerated as far as you can take it. Now let it get smaller and smaller until it almost disappears. Let someone else begin a new movement.

DOMINOES

Each person in the circle, create your own rhythmic movement that can be repeated. Keep it simple. Look to the right. When leader says change, switch to the movements of the person on the right. Repeat this until your own movement returns to you.

CHILDREN'S MOVEMENT GAME

One child leaves the room. Someone in the group will be designated as the initiator of a movement. The movement will be started and the child outside will be called in. When the child who is "it" isn't looking, the initiator will change the movement.

The initiator will continue changing the movement until the child who is "it" can guess who the initiator is.

PASS A MESSAGE

Let's all get into a circle and hold hands. (Joey), squeeze the hand of the person next to you. That person will then squeeze the next hand and so forth around the circle, until the squeeze comes back to (Joey). You may call it an energy squeeze.

Next we can pass hugs . . .
> kisses . . .
>> a compliment . . .
>>> hand shake . . .
>>>> or a back rub.

Think of some more good things to pass.

GENTLE SWAY

Kneel comfortably behind your partner. Person in front, sit relaxed with your legs outstretched or crossed, with eyes closed. Relax and trust your partner. Person in back, very gently and slowly take your partner's head between your hands. As slowly as possible move the head around. Even slower! Concentrate on taking care of your partner's head. Pay attention only to your partner. Your partner will feel this nurturing attention, or sense the lack of it. After about two minutes, slowly remove your hands. Gently lift one arm and softly, slowly move that arm. Person in front, give your arm over to your partner. Do not anticipate the movements, but allow yourself to be moved. Relax and enjoy it. Person in back, **after a few minutes** gently place the arm down. Do not let it drop. Work with the other arm for about another two minutes, and then with both arms.

See also Passive-Active, p. 110.

Reverse roles.

Verbally share your feelings with each other.

This is a totally calming and relaxing exercise.

SCULPTING

Sculpture can inspire the imagination. Make the impossible possible.
What can I be?
What can I do?
Where can I go?
What is possible for me?

What if I were a ballerina,
brave,
strong.

I would like to feel beautiful,
handsome,
gentle and loving,
successful.

Sculpting helps to dramatize situations.

I want to sculpt a perfect family for myself,
how I feel,
my favorite environment.

Using imagination is an ongoing open-ended process. Given a supportive environment, the possibilities for creative interaction and original, inventive ideas are endless.

TIME, SPACE AND LOCOMOTION

Can you walk around the room slowly and softly? . . . . .
> Freeze!

Good! Can you do that walking backwards? . . . .
> Freeze!

Yes! How about sideways? Let your arms also move from side to side . . . .
> Freeze!

Can you skip very high?
> Good! . . . .
> Freeze!

Can you jump in a low position?
> Very good! . . . .
> Freeze!

Run as fast as you can . . . .
> Freeze!

Can you move around the room in a very rounded, curved, soft form?
> Very nice! . . . .
> Freeze!

How about in a straight position? . . . . Walk as if you were made out of sticks.
> That's wonderful! . . .
> Freeze!

Continue in this way, using different combinations of locomotor movements: walk, run, skip, jump, hop, leap.
> ***Levels: high, medium, low.***
> > ***Time: quickly, slowly.***
> > > ***Shapes: round, straight.***
> > > > ***Direction: forward, backward, sideways.***

Your elbow is the lightest part of your body.

This will increase the student's range of variations to use in the other sculpture experiences.

Experiment with gravity to get interesting freeze positions.

Playing with the concept of gravity, what would happen to your hand if it were the lightest part of your body? To your head if it were the heaviest part of your body? Your stomach? Your elbow? Your backside as the lightest part?

Freeze these different positions. The signal for freezing can be the bang of a drum or other rhythm instruments.

LEVELS

High is all the space above your shoulders. It doesn't matter how tall or small you are. High is from the perspective of your own body.

Create a sculpture or statue on a high level. Make another sculpture or shape on a high level . . . . Another . . . A different one . . . . . Good!

The medium level is all the space between your shoulders and hips. Put one hand on your shoulder, and the other on your hip. Now, keeping your hands on the same level, move them out into the space in front of you. The space between your two hands is your medium level. Create a sculpture in that space no higher than your shoulder, and no lower than your hips. Change it . . . . . . Again! . . . . Another one . . . . Change . . . . . Yes, very good! . . . Relax!

Now all the space below your hips will be your low level. First create the boundary with your hand by placing your hand on your hip, and then extending it forward into space. Duck under your hand and create a low sculpture. Low does not have to be flat on the floor. There are many variations of low. Create another low sculpture . . . . and another . . . . . Very good!

Now get into groups of three and number yourselves "one", "two", and "three". All "ones" create a sculpture on a high level. All "twos" create a sculpture on a medium level. Make sure that one part of your body connects to your partner. All "threes" create a sculpture on a low level, attaching to one or both of your partners . . . Good! Now when I say "change", "ones" move to a medium level, "twos" to a low level, and "threes" to a high level, connecting to one or both partners . . . Change! Very Good! . . . When I say "change" again, move to the level you haven't been on yet. Yes . . . That's excellent!

This time when I say "Change", you decide nonverbally which level to move to. Your group sculpture will finish on three different levels. Don't forget to be connected. Change . . . Good! Again, change . . . yes, again, change . . . . They look wonderful!

We will now add flow, so that you will dance or flow gracefully from one position to the other. Beginning on a high level, let your body sway, flow softly into a medium level, and when you like your sculpture, freeze . . . Good! Now flow to a low level . . . A continuous, slow movement, till you get to a sculpture on a low level. Next will be the most difficult. Make as many movement adjustments as you need, to flow gracefully back up to a high position and freeze! Good!

We will now use music. Get back into your three levels. When I say "Change", you will flow to a different level. Make sure you stay nonverbal, and end up on three different levels . . . . Good! Change! . . . . . Change! . . . . Change! . . . .

Now each group will decide when it will want to change. Use your own timing. Remember to freeze each time.

Two groups of three may become a group of six. Create your sculpture on six different levels. Open your sculptures up. Make them large, but be sure to keep contact. Let's see all the shapes. Oh, they are marvelous. They are so beautiful!

I would like you to see each other.

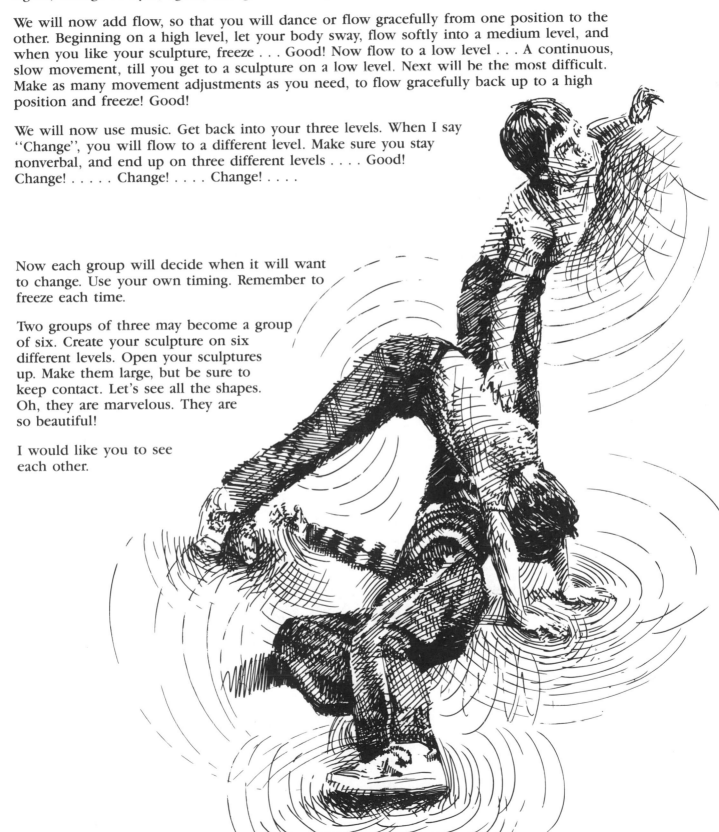

Let all but one group of six sit down and watch the flowing sculpture of the remaining group. While the one group is still dancing, ask another group of six to begin. When the second group is in motion, softly ask the first to observe. Continue until all groups have had a chance to perform. In this way the flow is continued even in changing groups.

Keep the last group to perform the one most in the center of the room. After the last group has performed, do not ask them to stop. Instead, ask two or three individuals from the other groups to simultaneously move over and attach to the group which is still in motion. After each new addition of people, ask the dancing group to change shapes. Reinforce the idea that everyone should try to be on a different level. Continue until the entire group is working together, still changing shapes. If it starts to look like a "hodgepodge", ask the group to spread out.

This is very effective, especially with inspiring music such as "Pas de deux" from the NUTCRACKER SUITE. It brings the entire group together in a dramatic and creative effort. I will very often end a session this way.

Being an active audience while others are performing is very important. Through your body language and facial expression you are giving your energy, positive feedback, and appreciation of the efforts of others. Your eyes, your smiles, the forward position of your body, your lack of talking to each other show the performers you are interested and appreciate their performance.

EXCHANGING SCULPTURES

Two groups of three will work together. Both sets of three will create their sculpture and remember it. They will then take turns teaching their sculpture to the other group, placing each person appropriately.

ELEVATOR

Use levels with 1-2-3, one being low and three being high, or 3-4-5 etc., emphasizing the lower number, medium number, and higher number.

Scramble the numbers 1-3 or 1-5. All start as low as possible. Slowly rise and stop at the level appropriate to your number, and attach to each other. Break apart. Scramble the numerals, and do it again. Say your numeral in order when the sculpture is final.

Do the same for syllables in words or names, or for sequencing letters in the alphabet.

REACH OUT AND TOUCH

We will walk throughout the space to the music "Reach Out and Touch". Keep changing your direction so that you avoid walking in a circle formation. Now one person may step into the center, form a sculpture, and freeze. Be aware of the sculpture from different perspectives as you continue to move around the room. Attach to the sculpture, one at a time, and freeze. Be aware of the entire group so that no more than one or two at a time will be attaching to the sculpture.

When it is finished, the first sculptor may initiate a movement impulse. A ripple effect will allow everyone to break away, moving again in different directions. Someone else may begin a new sculpture. Repeat this process until the end of the music with as many initiators as possible.

VARIATIONS
Extend the shape of the first sculpture. It does not have to be the same. It could be repeated on different levels with different body parts to emphasize the same feeling.

First sculpture can add a small movement such as a sway or bounce. This will be picked up in different ways in different body parts as each person attaches.

Each person can add his own sound as he attaches.

Choose a title such as Bridges, Tunnels, Outer Space, or Narrow Hallways. You name some.

Now create your sculpture story with your title in mind.

You can also dramatize poems or short stories.

HISTORICAL
FANTASY OR
CURRENT EVENTS

Working in sculptures on different levels, is a very good pre-story experience. This gives a background for working together, positive touching, group cooperation, and interesting configurations.

You may go into groups of six. Decide on an event, either current or historical. You will create three individual sculptures. The first is the beginning of the story, the second will be the middle, and the third is the ending. The rest of us will guess your story.

The performance of your story will be nonverbal, but you could add sound. Do not forget your different levels and connecting body parts. That will make your sculpture story visually interesting. Sometimes a small movement such as a sway or bounce is necessary to portray your story.

Have fun planning. It needn't take more than five or ten minutes at the most. After your story has been sculpted, you may perform it for the rest of the class.

The entire group could also create an original story. Begin by saying, "Once Upon a Time", and then continue. Different students will take their turns adding on until the story is finished. Try to keep it short. It may be real or nonsensical.

As many individuals as want to can play each role as it comes up in the story. Even objects can be portrayed such as, "the door opened". Instantaneously, one, two, or as many as want to can become a door. The story can be created first, and then acted out, or acted as it is being created.

It can be funny or serious, realistic or nonsensical, but it is always a fascinating process that allows for spontaneity, cooperation and dedication to the idea.

It is not necessary to give out character parts in advance. On-the-spot decisions of what role or roles to take keep the entire group actively interested and involved.

Creative storytelling can be stimulated by telling a fairy tale and asking the children to change it in a way they would like better.

Individual sculpture stories may be only one minute skits strung together to tell a longer story.

Take a real incident that happened in the classroom or school, and create a story around it. The facts are always allowed to change. Changing the ending to a story may be positive and even therapeutic.

Take an occasion such as someone's birthday, Thanksgiving, Halloween, etc. and create a story around that theme.

Use a group of vocabulary or spelling words and create a story with them.

A WISH

Who do you wish to be? A King? Queen? Superperson? What would that person do? How would you act? Where would you be? Create the environment using other students, and act out your fantasy.

SCULPTURE GYMNASTICS

Divide your group in half. Leave a large open space in the center. We will only work with one group. The other group will observe for the time being. One person from the first group, please come into the center and make a sculpture. Now, one at a time, attach yourselves to one or more in the sculpture, creating a new shape. The group will always be aware when someone is going into the sculpture, so that no more than one person attaches at a time. This awareness will be totally nonverbal. See the ongoing changes of your sculpture before becoming part of it. Be aware of making the sculpture large so that there are many types of empty spaces on different levels.

Make a shape that you will be able to hold for a few minutes. For example, standing on your toes or lifting one foot in the air, unsupported, may become too difficult to maintain. Also try to keep the different levels of high, medium, and low. Face different directions, so that there is no front or back to the sculpture . . . . That looks great!

Now the other group, circle around this sculpture. Notice all the shapes it makes: squares, triangles, rectangles, and others.

You can trace them with your hand. Good! Now look again at the sculpture from different angles and directions. What does it look like? Can you name it? Does someone have another idea of what this could be? Another name?

All names and ideas are accepted. They could be written on the chalkboard for later use. You can use these ideas for creative story telling. See Historical, Fantasy or Current Events, p. 106.

What spaces can you crawl under, move through, over, and around? Try it. Use this sculpture as a fantasy land to explore shapes. Move through slowly and gently so that you don't hurt the individuals making the sculpture.

Exploring the sculpture usually takes a minute or two before it collapses, often with a lot of laughter. Allow for a change of roles with the two groups.

BODY IMPULSE

Let one of your arms be the passive member of your body and the other one active. The active arm will mold and shape the hand, fingers, and total arm in different positions. Try this with other parts of your body. Let one hand be the puppeteer and the rest of your body the puppet.

MAKE IT A DANCE
Have one hand tap the other, setting it into motion and letting it go as far as it can. Then tap another part of your body such as your shoulder, hip, head, or other arm. Allow that movement to flow on, with the rest of the body giving in to it. The impulse starts a movement which is taken as far as it can go. Then you begin a new impulse. One movement flows into the next.

I remember experiencing this movement idea in a modern dance class with Karen Bamonte who performs and teaches modern technique in Philadelphia and Germany.

You may want to think of a quality or feeling such as your love, your talents, intelligence, or creative spirit, and take it into the world as far as it can possibly go.

This is done from a stationary place on the floor, using only personal space. See Personal Space, p. 21.

Tap your head . . . , your leg . . . Good! You select the next body part to move . . . . Keep it going.

PASSIVE-ACTIVE

One of you will be passive, the other active. Passive person, close your eyes and relax. You will need to trust your partner. Do not anticipate your partner's wishes. Allow yourself to be molded and moved.

Passive-Active was an often used improvisation at the Group Motion Studio in Philadelphia with Briggita and Manfred Fischbeck. No matter how many times I participated, it was always a different and successfully fun experience.

You need to be flexible enough to be sculpted, but not so relaxed that there is not enough firmness to sculpt.

Active person, take good care of your partner. Do not put your partner into positions that will be too difficult to hold or too uncomfortable. Treat your partner with care. Tell your partner by your touch that you are trustworthy.

Allow your imagination free play. Sculpt, move, energize your partner in gentle maneuvers. Tune in to your feelings. Respond to the music *if there is any.* Admire your sculpture, be with it, move with it, change it.

Partners change roles. Verbalize your feelings about the experience to each other.

TOTAL GROUP
Come into one circle to get ready for a group experience. Does anyone want to share with the group what you experienced and exchanged as partners . . . ?

This time those of you who would like to be passive, sit where you are and close your eyes. Those of you who want to be active, stand. The numbers of active and passive people do not have to be equal. Two or more active people can work with many passive people by grouping, sculpting, and creating scenes.

If you no longer want to be active, just sit down and close your eyes. A sculptor will come over to you. A passive person can change roles by opening her eyes and by beginning to sculpt other passive participants.

Enjoy yourselves. Change roles at any time and as often as you like. Be spontaneous with your sculpting. You may move from one passive person to another, or work with a few at a time. Remember to be nonverbal.

This experience can go on for a half hour or more. It will constantly change and evolve. Music with different rhythms and energies helps stimulate ideas and create an environment.

QUESTIONS FOR DISCUSSION
How did you feel being sculpted?

How did you feel sculpting?

Were you trusting with your partner?

Were there moments in which you were uncomfortable?

What did you particularly enjoy about this experience?

Was your partner easy to sculpt?

Did you feel tension in your partner's body? Just enough? Too much?

Which role did you prefer, passive or active? Why?

Sculpt your partner doing specific jobs in the community. Mold them into a fireperson, policeperson, traffic guard, etc. Others can guess who that person is.

FEELING SCULPTURE

Tune into how you are feeling right now. You might want to close your eyes to do this. Now look around the room and find someone who reminds you of this feeling. Be partners with this person.

Even though everyone is looking, participants generally find themselves with the right person.

Take turns sculpting your partner to look as you are feeling. Let your partner tell you how it makes her feel to be in that position. Share your feeling and see if they are the same. Let your partner sculpt you back into your feeling position. Do you still feel as you did originally? Discuss the feelings. Reverse roles.

One feeling may lead to another. Keep changing roles with your partner, sculpting these different feelings. Take some time to talk about how you felt.

This can easily lead to a group experience described in Passive-Active, p. 110.

FLOWING   HEALING   SCULPTING

Softly, gently allow your hands to move over your whole body as close as possible without touching. Move them over your head, face, shoulders, arms, torso, legs, in a continuing, flowing motion going from one part of your body to the next. Let your hands go to the part of your body that needs this healing energy. Your body will tell you. Don't think about it.

Move closer to one another. Give this beautiful healing energy to each other. Move from one person to the next, not in partners. Sense a continual flow of giving and receiving.

VARIATION

One person may stand in the center of ten people. The ten will give this flowing healing energy to the one in the center.

Work in groups of three. Two of you may work with the one partner. Change roles until all have had a chance in the center.

FAMILY SCULPTING

We are going to take a make-believe photograph of someone's family. Who would like to volunteer to pose the people in your immediate family for us?

Choose people from the class to stand in for your different family members. A male might remind you of a female family member, and vice versa. If you wish, you can interchange females, for male models. When you have your family together, put yourself in the picture. Don't forget the family pets.

QUESTIONS FOR OBSERVATION
Who are you next to? Was that the person you felt closest to at home? What can you observe about this family? Who was central? Who are the outsiders? Were there any? What else can you tell from this family photograph?

"This is my family at a picnic. My mother, father, sister, and myself. The dog, cat, and pet bird."

REFLECTIONS OF OTHER CHILDREN
"Nobody seems to be paying attention to anyone else." "No one is looking at each other." "They seem to be in their own world even though they are together, even the animals." "Sometimes families are like that."

CREATE YOUR IDEAL FAMILY
Now what would you like to change? Is there anybody you would like to remove altogether or place differently? Do that now . . . . Is there anyone you would like to add? More sisters or brothers? More animals?

I have done family sculpting with children as young as five years old. They sometimes have a tendency to put everyone in a straight line. Use some of the examples from the first sculpting activities to stimulate their spontaneity.

In one class, a child who was one of twelve children got rid of everyone. He didn't want anyone but himself in the sculpture. He really needed the space. In the same group a five-year-old girl, who lived only with her mother, wanted all the children in the group to become her brothers and sisters.

Done without intensity, this experience has been consistently enjoyable and therapeutic for all ages. In my experience such flexibility of choice brings a positive response. Since no judgments are made, children know they can always bring back, rearrange, and add to family members.

VARIATIONS
Mold your family members as if they were clay. Have them do different things in the family room, dining area, outdoors at a special event, the backyard, a party, a picnic, at the zoo. You decide.

Once posed, children may comment on what they observed and what they feel is happening.

PARENT CHILD

Child will sculpture parent(s) or the models of parent(s) in the position in which she would like them to be. She then places herself in with the sculptured parents. Let the child verbalize what the sculpture means to her.

HOW DO YOU WALK IF

You are on clouds?
The house is on fire?
Your leg is broken?
You are waist high in water?
You are in snow or mud?
You are going down hill?
You are on a narrow ledge?
You are on a dark deserted street?
You are a tightrope walker?
You are on glue?
You are holding something
hot and full?

You are in heavy traffic?
You are on hot sand?
You are trying not to be seen?
The room is rocking?

You are on
Quick sand,
Eggs,
Glass,
A picket fence,
Grass,
Someone's back,
Rocks crossing a brook,
An oily floor,
A vacant lot with obstacles?

YOU MAKE UP SOME MORE

OBSERVATIONS
Observe each other walking. Tell what you see, such as light,
heavy, strong, fast, slow, flowing, bouncy, straight, holding
weight forward or back, etc. Encourage "movement"
rather than "feeling" descriptions.

116

A statement can also be used to stimulate individual and group sculptures such as:

You just won a million dollars!

You got a flat tire on a rainy day!

I saw you break that window!

Someone is following you down a dark street!

A surprise birthday party is given for you!

YOU MAKE SOME UP

Create sculptures and sculpture stories using your shadows on a large blank wall. See Shadow Play, p. 184.

CREATING ENVIRONMENTS

Make moving sculptures as part of a special
environment. For example, let's create a busy
city street. What types of things would you find?
Traffic lights,
  Sign posts,
    Tall buildings,
      Cars,
        Trucks,
          Food carts.

What are the people doing?
  Do they walk fast or slow?
    What kind of people do you see?
    Parents and children.
    People in business suits walking briskly.
    Panhandlers or bums slouching against buildings.
    People looking into store windows,
        Talking,
          Laughing,
            Angry,
              Children jumping rope.
  Someone yelling from a soap box.
    Sirens and horns blasting.
      A street fight.
        What else can you think of?

Be the different things and people.
Think about how they move and
what kind of sounds they make.
Let the feelings of this environment
go through your entire body.

WEATHER CONDITIONS

How would you move if it were very cold? Would your body be
open or closed? Do a cold dance. How would you move if you
were hot? If it were raining? Windy? A blizzard? How would
you move if you were chest-high in water?

Create a dance out of these movements. Have others guess by your
movements what kind of weather conditions there are.

*In Sarah Chapman's Children's Dance class at
Temple University we divided the room up
in three sections. One being a city, one a
jungle, and one a desert. We then all moved
through the different sections, simulating
parts of the environment.*

DIVIDE THE GROUP IN HALF
Half the class will be the environment, such as a thick forest. Create many different shapes on different levels and directions, being the trees, bushes, etc. The other half will move through this created space as themselves, insects, or animals. Be aware of the spaces. Are they large or small? How can you move in a thick forest? Do you have to move slowly or quickly? Do you have to get on different levels? Be aware of needing to go under branches or around bushes.

ON A BOAT

Other Environments

A circus	A supermarket
The zoo	Our planetary system
The desert	The beach
Jail	A jungle

CREATE A STORY, ADD SOUND, ADD PROPS, ASK QUESTIONS

What would you see in one of these environments? How would all of these be moving? What would they be doing? What are the weather conditions? Would the movements be fast or slow, light or strong?

FEELINGS IN DIFFERENT ENVIRONMENTS
Be in your different environments feeling grumpy, sad, silly, sleepy, snobbish, happy, bashful, angry. You add some more! How would you act with these feelings in different places? Have the group guess what you're feeling.

MACHINES

Making machines can be a great deal of fun. Begin in a way similar to Sculpture Gymnastics, p. 108.

Everyone may move around the outside of the circle, walking in different directions. Leave a large empty space in the middle. One person may begin by entering the center, creating machine-like movements. You don't have to know what part of the machine you are or what kind of a machine you are beginning to create. Just make a simple, repeatable movement.

Now another person, coordinate your machine-like movement with the first machine part so that your movements are synchronized.

Continue in this manner until everyone is making his own movements, all working together to create one huge machine.

NAME IT
Do it again . . . . this time add a special sound to go along with your movement.

IN SMALL GROUPS OF FIVE
Create a machine or gadget you might find in the house, such as a toaster, clothes-washer, vacuum, telephone, typewriter, can opener, clock. Add some more to this list.

Perform this machine for the rest of the class and we will guess what you are.

INDIVIDUAL MACHINES
Create any machine you can think of, real or imaginary. We will guess what you are. Use all possible body parts as your gears.

MACHINES AND BIOLOGY

THE DIGESTIVE SYSTEM

Using the same techinque as household gadgets, we can explore parts of the human body such as the digestive track.

One or a few of us can be a piece of food. Some of us will be teeth chopping up the food. What kind of movements will the food make as it is being chopped up? Then the food will glide down the esophagus into the stomach. Here the gastric juices will churn us more. What will the food do here? How will it look?

The food could now divide into different categories. Some becoming energy for the entire body, some becoming fat cells, and some leaving as waste. Decide what function you will have and what shape and movement you'll take as you go down your pathway.

What kind of sounds would you be making?

Try the same technique with other functions of the body such as:

       Bloodstream . . .
         Heart . . .
            Eyes . . .
               Ears . . .
                  How oxygen travels . . .
                 Lungs . . .

What others would you like to add?

Using yarn, lay out the different organs of the body. Jump in and out of the different parts.

See Patterning, p. 56.

ART AND MOVEMENT

All visual art works can be interpreted in movement. You can discuss lines in terms of hard, soft, sharp,
 heavy, light, straight,
  curved, spiral, zigzag,
   large or small, and direction.

Other qualities that can be interpreted with movement in space are color,
 intensity,
  light and shadow,
   cold and hot,
    focus,
     shapes,
      and feelings.

Art has movement, movement can be art, a sculpture in space and time.

MACHINES AND SPONGE PAINTING

In groups of four, sit around one very large piece of paper with a set of tempera paints, scissors, and sponges for each group. Use a small piece of paper to cut or tear a shape that resembles a gear, wheel, or other machine part. It can be totally imaginary. Number one person in each group, place your paper shape on the large paper and sponge paint around its edges. Number two person, connect your shape to the first, and sponge paint around it. Number three and four persons, take your turns connecting to the shapes already there. Repeat this process as many times as you wish until you feel your painting is finished.

Hang these marvelous designs around the room.

CHOREOGRAPH YOUR PAINTINGS

Gather around and observe them. What direction is your gear going? Diagonal, circular, up, down. What shape is it? How is it interacting with the other gears? Is it smooth or jagged? Where is the focus of the painting?

Incorporate these qualities in your body. In cooperation with the rest of your foursome, create in space what you have done on paper. These can be short two-minute choreographs, or as long as you wish.

Perform them for each other.

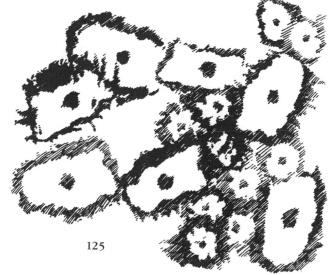

After one of my
workshops, Marilyn
Ross, artist and
elementary art
teacher, expanded
the machine
experience into a
sponge painting
lesson for her
special classes.
I then reinterpreted
it back into
movement.

The above sponge painting was interpreted
by the students as moving in a spiral
direction, round, and focusing toward the
center.

126

STRING PAINTING WITH LEVELS

Find a partner and get the following materials: Two pieces of string about two or three feet long, two jars with different colors of tempera paint, and one large sheet of paper at least two by three feet.

Fold your drawing paper in half and reopen it. Take turns with the following process. Dip your string into your chosen color of paint, holding on to one end. Carefully place the painted string on only one half of the paper, creating some kind of design. Let the dry end stick off the paper. Fold the other half of the paper over the string. While your partner puts some body weight on the paper, pull out your string. The second partner can then repeat the process using a different color of paint on top of the first design.

The result will be a beautiful two color butterfly effect with one color being underneath the other. Try this with music.

We are now going to dance our painting. Be aware of the level you want to be on. Notice the shapes, direction, and focus your design takes. See how your two colors relate to each other. In cooperation with your partner, choreograph the string painting in space.

I first remember doing this string painting experience in 1957 with Gladys Andrews Fleming, Creative Movement professor, and Dr. Montgomery, Art professor in one of my classes at New York University.

BODY PARTS COLLAGE

WARMUP

Find all the possible ways your fingers can move, stretching, clasping, wiggling, relating to each other. Good! Keep finding new ways.

Now elbows. They are sharp and angular. Find all the ways elbows move, bend, straight, pointing in, out, up, down. Good!

Now the entire arm. Make beautiful patterns in the air as if you are carving the air like clay. Nice and large, soft, sharp, behind you, in front and above, below you. Now move them in a new way. Create something you've never done before. Beautiful!

How about your shoulders? Up, down, forward, backward, alternately rolling them. Keep finding new ways to move those marvelous shoulders. They sometimes carry heavy burdens. Let's free them. Good!

Now your head and neck. Side to side, back and forth, roll your head, stretch your neck. Keep finding another way. Good!

Now your back, stomach, and waist. Slowly bend and twist in all directions, ripple your back and stomach . . . . Try another way . . . . Good! How about your hips?

Lie down so you can put your legs in the air. Begin with toes, feet, then knees. Whole legs. Yes, that is fine!

Now stand up and move the entire body as you go through the room. When you encounter others, relate to them with arms, legs, or hands. Create a dance with them for a few moments and move on to the next.

COLLAGE

With the help of a partner, trace your individual body parts and combination of body parts such as hands, arms and hands, feet, legs, torso, head. After drawing them in different positions, color and cut them out. On a huge sheet of paper we will place and paste these body parts in some form of design. Let your imagination run free. Allow it to take its own form.

Does the collage tell a body story? Choreograph this story, recreating in space what you imagine the different body parts would be doing, and how they would move.

LINES AND DRAWING

Everyone choose your own personal space. Using your arms and hands, draw a pattern in space until you find one you can repeat. When you like what you have, repeat it over and over again with different body parts, head, foot, shoulder, elbow, hand, and so on. Keep your pattern simple.

With charcoal and large newsprint, close your eyes and recreate your line pattern in drawing. Use the hand you don't normally use to do this. Get the feel of it. You may go over and over it. The feeling of this pattern is already in your body. Just let it flow out onto the paper. It does not have to be exact.

Draw again on another paper with your eyes open using the hand you normally use for writing or drawing.

We're now going to pin up everyone's drawings around the room. Walk around and look at everyone's patterns. How many different types of lines are there? Long-short, strong-delicate, straight-curved, thick-thin, dark-light, angular-horizontal-vertical.

Anyone who wants to may now take a turn creating his line drawing in space using the entire body. The rest of us will be an appreciative audience. Allow your body to respond to the different types of lines you drew.

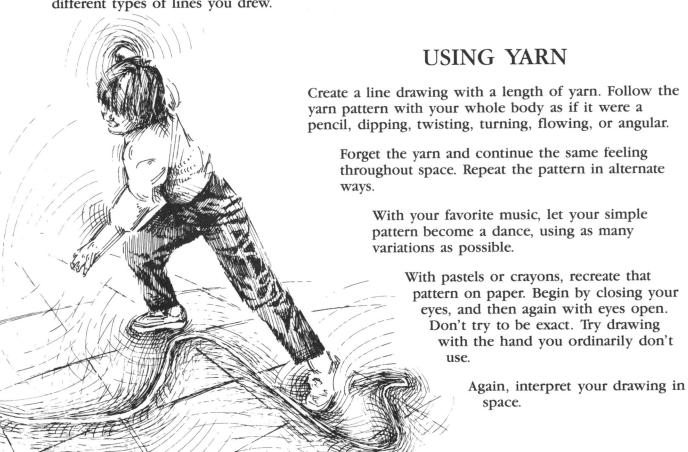

USING YARN

Create a line drawing with a length of yarn. Follow the yarn pattern with your whole body as if it were a pencil, dipping, twisting, turning, flowing, or angular.

Forget the yarn and continue the same feeling throughout space. Repeat the pattern in alternate ways.

With your favorite music, let your simple pattern become a dance, using as many variations as possible.

With pastels or crayons, recreate that pattern on paper. Begin by closing your eyes, and then again with eyes open. Don't try to be exact. Try drawing with the hand you ordinarily don't use.

Again, interpret your drawing in space.

NEGATIVE
AND
POSITIVE
SPACES

Form groups of six, eight, or ten. Half of each group may create a sculpture. Be sure to hold your shape while you are attached to one or two of your partners on different levels and at different body parts. Make your sculpture as large as possible so that there is lots of negative space between you.

The other half of the group, slowly walk around the sculpture seeing the new shapes and also the shapes created by the empty spaces. Which space attracts you? . . . Put your body into it, fill up the empty space . . . . Shape yourself into the new environment that was created for you. What form are you in?

NOTE: Use of the words "positive" and "negative" space do not have any value judgements. In this exercise "positive" means occupied space. "Negative" means unoccupied space.

Very carefully leave the structure so as not to disturb what was created by the second group . . . . Be flexible . . . . Let go of your shape. You will come back to it in yet another way . . . . Walk around, see the new sculpture and new spaces left . . . . What appeals to you? . . .

In slow motion re-enter this new world. Try out this environment. Find different ways of fitting your body into these newly created shapes. Changing and rechanging. Creating and recreating.

The second group, again in slow motion, leave the environment with its newly formed shapes.

This is an ongoing process of leaving and re-entering, constantly reshaping your body, seeing new negative and positive shapes.

Repeat about ten times or as long as interest allows, or for the length of a musical piece.

RELATED IDEAS

SCIENCE
Discuss the constant changing and rechanging of the seasons. Notice the negative and positive spaces such as the impressions made by fossils in rocks.

MATHEMATICS
Experiment with "volume". All the space will be taken up in the formed shapes.

BALANCE

Hold your partner's hands or wrists securely. You will be balancing each other's weight by pulling in the opposite direction and bending your knees.

Keep making adjustments as you support and balance each other. Vary your balancing dance by holding only one hand. Use different levels and positions, twisting and turning as you do.

Trust your partner, and be trustworthy.

Sit facing each other. Hold hands and be a see-saw together, balancing back and forth.

Sit back-to-back and try to stand by pushing against each other. Play elevator, going up and down this way, maintaining back pressure. Do the same with groups of four, back-to-back with another group of four. The line of four may link arms. The only contact the two rows have with each other is from back pressure. One person may give the signal to begin.

Our senses are constantly responding to our environment in order to keep our balance. For example, if our sense of sight is gone, the other senses will intensify to compensate. Our physical body is also making constant adjustments so that we keep our balance.

Begin in a curled up position with as much of your body touching the floor as possible. Very slowly get higher and higher, ending with as little of your body touching the floor as possible. Return slowly down to a relaxed position.

What happened to your balance as you got higher, with less of your body touching the floor?

What happened to your balance as you got lower, with more of your body touching the floor?

One person, pose three or more individuals in a balanced sculpture.

Use mirroring to create the feeling and look of balance. Find a position where one side of your body mirrors the other side. Explore with different movements, always mirroring yourself. Try this in different positions, such as lying down, kneeling or sitting. Travel through space, still mirroring. Now move asymmetrically where one arm may be up and the other down. Reach in all directions and on all levels. Move around the room, sometimes on a high and then low level.

Work in pairs, trying different positions, one person balancing the other. Use different levels and directions.

Make symmetrical and asymmetrical sculptures balancing each other.

BALANCE IN: ART
Fold a paper in half. Cut a design on the open side. Open it to find the perfect balance in its mirror image.
Create a balanced design using pastels and paper.
Discuss what is balancing it and what it might need to become more balanced. Try this in a different media: clay, found objects, blocks.

MATHEMATICS
Create a balance beam with blocks, showing how different weights can be equal. This can lead to lessons on equal and unequal sets.

SCIENCE
Discuss the balance of nature.

SOCIAL STUDIES
Discuss the balance, or give and take in relationships.

"How many ways can you move while balancing on one foot?"

ART SCULPTING AND DRAPING WITH CREPE PAPER

Find a partner. One of you will shape into a sculpture, sitting or standing, that you can hold for a period of time. The other partner will drape and totally wrap you, using a roll of crepe paper. Be careful not to tear the paper since the uninterrupted line creates the boundaries of the sculpture.

Don't forget your camera for this one!

Observe your wrapped sculpture. Notice the shapes, lines and boundaries. What does it remind you of? (Besides a mummy, of course.)

Can you name it?

It is wonderful to have a full length mirror in front of each sculpture so the children can see themselves.

Sculpture, notice how it feels to be wrapped.

LARGER GROUPS
Four or more may create a sculpture. The rest of you, use different colors of the rolled crepe paper to wrap them.

Weaving

Some of you may position yourselves at different places throughout the room in sculptured positions on all levels.

Sculptors, slowly and carefully decide which materials to choose. Flow through the room, draping sculptures and connecting them with the materials. ***You will have an environment completely draped and sculpted.***

When you are finished, you may do a slow motion dance, weaving under-over-around and through the room.

Other Boundaries

PERSONAL BOUNDARIES
How far can you reach into space from a stationary position? This is your personal boundary. Draw an imaginary line around you. That is your boundary line. **See Personal Space, p. 21.**

Close your eyes. Now feel the outlines of your face, nose, eyes, mouth, hairline, hair. Trace it gently with your fingers, now down your neck and entire body. **See Feeling Shapes, p. 68.**

Do this in partners, tracing each other's body boundaries. **Stimulate body boundaries as in Self Massage, p. 52.**

GEOGRAPHY
Discuss the boundaries that divide nations and states.

MATH AND LANGUAGE
Feel the boundaries of cut out letters, numbers, and shapes.

SAFETY
Talk about the boundaries for crossing streets, for cars and pedestrians.

SOCIAL STUDIES
Discuss rules and regulations (spoken and unspoken) for social boundaries.

How close is it permissible to be next to someone? When is it bad manners to make eye contact? When is it important to make eye contact? When are you invading someone else's boundaries?

The answers will differ from culture to culture.

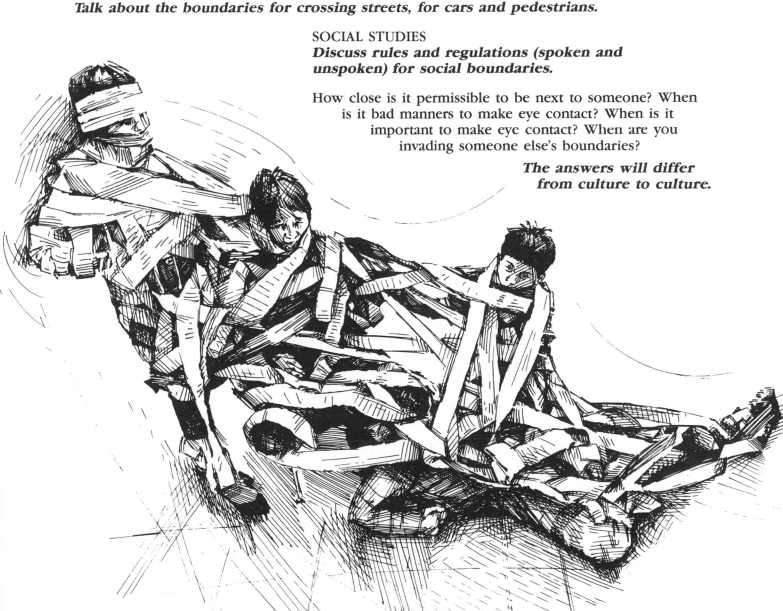

PARACHUTE SCULPTING

VARIATIONS
Use different types of material for draping. A parachute is wonderful for this. Let it float on top of the individuals that are creating the sculpture, falling where it may. Walk around and name the shape. You could also use streamers, scarves, shawls, yarn, bolts of material, and whatever you'd like to add.

SCULPTING WITH PIPECLEANERS

Create the sculptures you have made with your body with pipe cleaners. Put them in different environments, attaching them on different levels or positioning them for individual stories.

These pipe cleaner sculptures can then be recreated into body sculptures and stories.

SHADOW DRAWING

Create shadow sculptures by standing behind a large sheet with a light source behind you. Others draw or trace these shapes.

To extend or expand the sculptured designs, add props such as sticks, scarves, or large material for draping.

Use different types of music to inspire the shapes and formations being sculpted.

"It's a Brigantine Castle!"

"It's Mount Everest!"

"It's a volcano!"

"It's the bottom of an ice cream cone!"

"It's a triangle!"

A SCULPTURE MUSEUM

Walk around the museum, silently looking at the different sculptures. After a while go back to the one you liked best. Let your mind be flooded with all the possibilities of why you like a particular sculpture. We will now go as a group and visit each other's statue. Get into the same pose as your statue. Feel what it's like to be this new person. Say what you are doing or where you are going. Where did you come from? Who are you? What are you feeling? When you have an image of who you are as this sculpture, begin to move as this new person or shape. Continue the movement story of your sculpture in space.

Write about yourself as this sculpture. Give it a background. What happened and what will happen? Give your story an ending.

Group together in threes and share the details of your life as a sculpture.

The above illustration is of a sculpture by Claire Colinet called "Ankara Dancer".

BACK IN THE CLASSROOM
Think of one phrase and a few movements that would best describe your statue. Come to the center, one at a time, and share your sculpture story.
or
One at a time come to the center and strike your one pose, saying your descriptive phrase. The next person, if you can add to the story, attach to the first person and say your phrase. As many as possible, add to the story by attaching your sculpture to the others.

You may want to do some sculpture experiences first as warm-ups. See pgs. 101-111.

Try extending this experience by creating your sculpture in clay.

If you can't get to the museum, bring small sculptures to the classroom, or bring slides or photographs of sculptures. With slides you can also shape your shadow in with the picture projected from the slide. See Shadow Play, p. 184.

A fourth grade boy interpreting the sculpture "Ankara Dancer" said, "I was searching for a solution to my problem." He continued the story creating another pose (see illustration at right) and said, "I found the solution and felt much better."

MURALS

Begin with a warmup, moving all your different body parts. *See Collage, p. 128.* Let's choose a theme such as Spring. Using music that makes us think of Spring, we will dance throughout the room, incorporating as much of our body as possible. *Use a few Spring words from Words with a Theme, p. 78, to create a dance of:*

> *Opening*
>> *Stretching*
>>> *Swooping and*
>>>> *Closing.*
>>>>> *Repeat these words many times.*

Mural paper is up around the walls of the room with crayons, pastels, and magic markers available.

With the feeling of spring in our bodies, you may go to any section of the paper and draw what you feel. It may be real, make believe, large or small, however you wish to express it. The music will continue throughout the entire art activity.

What were some of your feelings and ideas as you drew? Let's create a Spring story based on these feelings and ideas and then we'll recreate it in movement.

PORTRAITS

This experience can be used after any dance activity.

Each of you take a large sheet of paper and some pastels. You may draw a portrait of yourself. This portrait will be a result of your feelings, not artistic ability . . . . Print one or two word descriptions of your self-drawing. Give it a title.

Leave it on the floor while we move about the room discovering all the different self-drawings. Notice how each is different.

Go back to your own portrait and feel what you drew. Let yourself feel the portrait in your body. Begin to dance the feeling of your portrait. Everyone may do this together . . . . *Everyone dancing together can lessen inhibitions.*

Let's make a large circle. We will show your portraits one at a time. Give its title and share your dance of what you drew for everyone.

FEET PATTERNS

Trace the children's feet on paper and have them cut out the shapes. Arrange them on the floor in different patterns. Use lively music and follow the feet, making different patterns by using different pathways. This can be our foot dance.

You may number the feet patterns as a game to reinforce numerals.

You may also have large sheets of paper on the floor, and create foot prints by painting the bottoms of your feet and then dancing. Oh! What a mess! This will definitely need careful cleanup preparations.

BODY TRACING

Lightly trace the outline of your partner's body. Alternate roles three times, changing shapes and positions.

For those who do not want to be touched, direct your partner to trace your body by placing her hands as close as possible without actually touching. Close your eyes. You will still feel the warmth of her hands as your body is traced.

Now taking turns, trace each other on paper with crayon. When your outlines are finished, close your eyes and tune into your feelings. How do you feel at this very minute?

Open your eyes . . . . Choose crayons and color your own outline with designs, pictures, words, or just scribbling that expresses these feelings.

These body outlines can be drawn on after many different movement experiences over a period of hours or days. This is a fun experience for children of all ages, five through adult. The very young may need adult help in tracing and cutting their body outline. Music while tracing and drawing can be used.

Cut out your outline and hang it up in the room.

Who is this person? Can you verbalize some of those feeling designs? Begin with I am . . . I feel . . . I can . . . I want . . . .

Take some time to choreograph your designs. You will each have a chance to dance your picture for the whole group and verbally share your feelings about this experience.

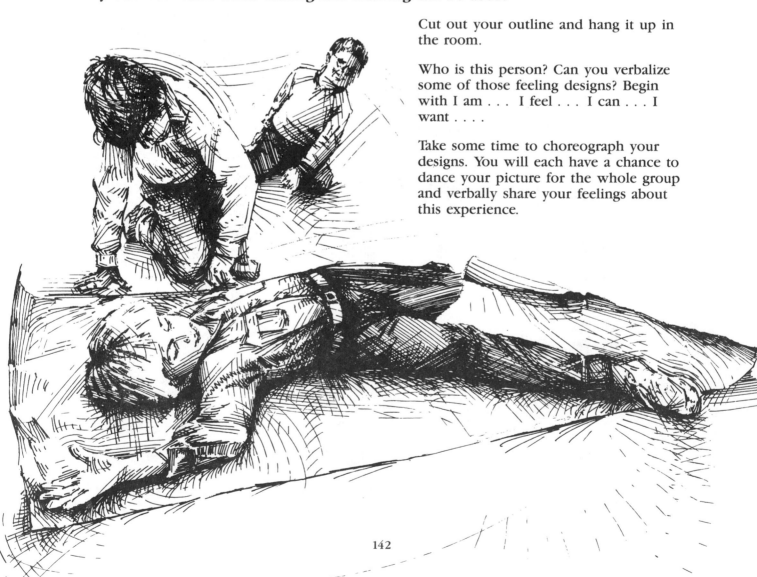

MUSIC AND MOVEMENT

Music can be interpreted in movement and movement into music. Begin with either one. It can enhance the movement experience,
    Make your feelings soar,
      Soothe you,
        Stimulate your fantasies,
        And be healing.

GIBBERISH

Gibberish is a non-language language. It is a combination of sounds formed to make words without meaning. It usually is accompanied by a great deal of intonation, facial expression and gesture.

In partners, have an argument in gibberish.

In a group of five or six, first person begins a story, next one adds to it, and so on. Exaggerate your expression. Ask yourself what this story was about.

Use gibberish in an "invented" party. Walk around the room, talking to different people individually and in small groups. You don't necessarily need to know what you are saying. Ideas come up in this spontaneously created language. Once they do, you can expand them.

This is also a very good loosening up activity for creative writing.

EXAMPLE
A fourth grade class created the following conversations for this gibberish experience.

"I really need some help."
"Of course I'll help you."

"For me?"
"Yes, it's from my heart."

"Get out of here!"
"Make me!"
"No, you did it!"

RHYTHM INSTRUMENTS

You can buy rhythm instruments, but making your own is very simple. Choose wooden spoons, sandpaper, hand egg beater, boxes, cans with pebbles inside, sticks, pots and pans, etc.

Rhythm instruments may accompany a dance or you can create a dance by responding to the sound of the rhythm instruments.

Have a conversation with a partner. Take turns "talking" to your partner, using different rhythmic patterns. *See Conversations, p. 88.*

How does the sound of a triangle, a drum or rhythm sticks make you want to move?

MUSIC QUALITIES

Listen to the pitch. Is it high? Create movement on a high level. Is it low? Create movement on a low level. ***Choose music with a variety of pitch.*** Move through the room responding to the different levels. Involve your whole body, and make it a dance. Now listen to a simple melody, and respond in space to its various levels of pitch.

Listen for intensity.

Is it light ***treble*** or is it heavy ***bass***?

Staccato or sustained?

Loud or soft?

Fast or slow?

Discover movement phrases that reflect these qualities. Combine a few of them in response to a particular piece of music. Try different combinations such as slow, light, sustained.

PATTERNING A STAFF

Pattern a staff on the floor. ***See p. 60.*** While someone plays notes on a piano or xylophone, follow the notes by going up and down on the pattern. Begin simply.

Place one octave on the floor beginning with Middle C. Walk or jump the letters in response to the musical instrument.

Jump onto the letters ***notes*** to make simple words such as:

fad	dad	cab
bed	cafe	face
bad	gab	ace.

Using different locomotor movements, move to the different notes.

Change the qualities, using different levels, time or flow.

DANCES FROM DIFFERENT LANDS

We are going to make up our
own dances to the music from
different lands. While we won't
perform the traditional steps to
these ethnic dances, the ones
we choreograph will still have
the flavor of that country, and a
feeling of authenticity.

Let the music lead you.
How does it invite you to
move? With strong or
light movements?
Down toward the
earth or up high
toward the sky?
Fast or slow?
Would your
gestures be
expansive or
restricted?
Are you telling
a story?

What are you wearing?
Boots,
Bouffant pants,
Billowy skirt,
Ribbons and flowers,
Do you have bare feet?

Are you using any props?
Scarves,
Sticks,
Streamers,
Castanets,
Tambourines?

**You may want to refer to pictures of dancers
in their native dress.**

What does your environment look like? Are you
outdoors? Indoors?
On grass? In a tremendous hall?

Just experiment and enjoy yourselves.

The following are some suggestions you may wish to incorporate.

AFRICA
Strong direct movements. Use of drums, rattles.
INDIA
Intricate hand movements. Small foot stamps. Bells.
VIENNA
Waltz. Large flowing movements around the room.

AMERICA: NATIVE
Small, stamping movements and circle formations, accompanied by gourds, drums, and bells.
SPAIN
Large skirts, cumberbunds with tight pants. Hard shoes. Hold upper body erect. Large controlled arm movements and quick small steps.
ADD YOUR OWN.

MUSIC LEVELS

By utilizing the "Levels" experience, p. 102, we can explore high, medium and low notes.

Let's harmonize. The person sculpting on a high level begin by singing "La" on a high note. The person sculpting on a medium level follow by singing "La" on a medium note. The third person, flow right in, attaching to one or both partners creating a sculpture on a low level, while singing on a low note.

Now move apart in silence. Alternate with medium first, then high, then low. Make other combinations. Let the sculpture stay as long as the third voice lasts.

Then gently flow apart and come together in a different combination, always creating a new sculpture and a new sequence of sound.

Try it with eight people, each one being a different note.

```
                              Do
                           Ti
                        La
                     Sol
                  Fa
               Me
            Re
         Do
```

Create an eight level sculpture. Sing your note as you move into the sculpting space and connect. After the last person is in, sing your scale again one at a time. Fini!

Try mixing up the notes as you come into the sculpture. Try a simple tune. Make up your own tune.

MUSICAL LEVELS FOR THE YOUNGER CHILD
Place your hand in front of you, hip level. As we listen to the eight notes of the scale move your hand up for each note. Now let's listen to the notes as they go down. Move your hand accordingly.

Use your whole body. Start very low for the first note. Raise yourself higher for each note as you move up the scale. Let's do it again. This time we will also use our voice in tune with the note. Up then down. Good!

MIRRORING
Respond to music going up or down. Follow each other. Move through the room mirroring each other. ***See Mirroring, p. 84.***

WORD SOUNDS

Respond in movement to such words as roaring, banging, whispering, laughing, sobbing, sneezing.

HISSING

LOVING

LISTENING

Barbara Mettler has a wonderfully large selection of movement words in her book *MATERIALS OF DANCE.*

CHANTING

Use a chant you know or make up your own. Ommmmmmm is a very well known one. Any of the vowel sounds can become a chant. The longer the period of time you use a chant, the more powerful it becomes.

ORCHESTRATED MOVEMENT GAME

One person make any kind of movement. The rest of the group create a sound in response. Dancer, continue creating an orchestrated piece.

Two people stand opposite each other, creating movements in conversation, taking turns. The rest of the group will put sound to it.

FOUND SOUNDS

Found sounds are from all the things you can find in the room or in your pockets that can make a sound. For example a comb, keys, coins rattling, paper tearing or crumpling, a pen opening and closing, something banging. You add some more to this list.

Experiment with these sounds in one large group or in smaller groups. Put your sounds together in a repeatable way. In small groups record your found sound orchestration. Choreograph some movements to your recorded sounds.

Your choreography does not have to be more than two or three minutes long. Show off your dance to the rest of the class.

CONVERSATIONS

In partners, first person, sing a short melodic line. Second person, answer with a short melodic line or phrase. Have a back and forth conversation. Add a gesture or full movement to the music phrase. This could take the form of question or answer.

RHYTHMS

Work in partners. First person, clap or stamp out a rhythm. Partner, answer this rhythm with your own pattern and continue the conversation. Let more and more of your body get involved. Begin to move throughout the room. Afterward, discuss the experience.

BODY SOUNDS

Try tongue clicking,
  Clapping,
    Stamping,
      Snapping fingers,
        Hands rubbing body,
          Slapping different body parts,

Other mouth sounds:
  Teeth clicking,
    Lips smacking,
      Humming.

Begin by experimenting with all of them. What other body sound can you make?

One person, begin with your chosen sound. One at a time each of you join in with your sound in rhythm. *A spontaneous orchestration will evolve.*

Extend this experience by moving throughout the room, responding to your own sound. Use a "Follow the Leader" technique as individuals begin different movements and sound. Use the whole space and different directions.

This activity was stimulated by a dance concert of Zero Moving Dance Company in Philadelphia, PA.

SILENCE

Silence can be an important alternative to music and sound. In silence you are free to focus inward and respond to your own heartbeat, pulse, or feelings. All the experiences in this book where music is suggested can also be done in silence.

FANTASY

In fantasy we are free to try out feelings, ideas, hopes and skills which we may be afraid to really use. We can be as tiny, gigantic, strong or vulnerable as we want. We are able to accomplish the most incredible feats or become any character, real or fictional. We can look at the world or ourselves upside down or inside out, become parts of machines, get inside objects or bodies, and go to all the imagined places of the world.

There are no limitations on fantasy so let your mind create anything and everything. Let all possibilities exist. Bring fantasy a little closer to reality by putting it into movement.

Movement can be the bridge between fantasy and reality. The beginning of dreams coming true . . . .

FANTASY ENVIRONMENTS

Lie down on your backs . . . totally relaxed with eyes closed. Think of an object. Any object . . . small or large, hard or soft. Anything . . . Now I want you to imagine some way of entering this object. This is fantasy, so it doesn't matter if the object is smaller than you, or if it doesn't have a natural opening. You create some way to get inside.

Now that you are inside, look around (in your mind's eye). What shape is it? Allow your body to form that shape. How does it feel inside? Hard or soft? Wet or dry? Rough or smooth? Cool or warm? What colors do you see? How does it smell? What would it sound like if you tap it? Can you stand up in it? Can you roll, wiggle, stretch, twist, turn, rock, sit up? How much can you move? What does it look like on the inside? Is there anyone else with you? Feel its shape with your body. Is it dark or light?

I'll ask you to explore it awhile by yourselves without asking you any more questions . . . .

Now get ready to leave. Look for a way. It could be the same way you entered, or it could be another way out. You may actually move your body as you find your way out, and then open your eyes. Use imagination.

Who would like to share what object he was in and how it felt? What was the experience like? How did you get in and out? Was it comfortable?

This can be done with a specific object for the whole class such as an egg or cocoon, a flower or rock, a pencil or light bulb, etc. Just let your imagination go wild. Ask questions relating to the five senses and types of movements one could possibly make while inside this object. Some children may need more time than others to work themselves out of the object.

THINGS TO WATCH OUT FOR
A young child might be afraid of the dark, and he will tell you his object was dark inside. Tell him to flick on a switch to turn on a light. If it's too cold tell her to imagine special clothing that will keep her warm. We want to make sure this is a positive experience.

In an adult class, a man imagined himself in a marshmallow. He had trouble getting out, so the whole class helped him. First we all ate some of the marshmallow and then we literally helped him by pulling him through.

These fantasies can take on a reality of their own and MUST be treated seriously, carefully, and with loving support.

INSECTS

Think of an insect you don't like, that makes you squirm . . . really yuk. Let me see the reaction in your body, in your face. Good! Now close your eyes. Take three deep slow breaths. Pay attention to your breathing, and feel yourself relax more with each breath. Now think of your insect. See its shape and how it moves. What is its texture? Fuzzy? Slimy? Does it have legs? Wings? Does it move slowly? Quickly? Does it have color? Make a sound?

Allow your hands to feel the quality of your imaginary insect. Feel with your arms, toes, legs, your whole body. Allow your face to feel the expression of this insect. Now with your eyes still closed, begin to move in place with the feelings of this insect. Now using soft focus, **eyes open but lowered** move through the space with these feelings. Be the insect, feel the insect's feelings, move its movements.

As you come across another insect you may want to interact with it in some way, and then move on. **Let this continue as long as there is interaction and interest.**

Each person, be your insect alone and the rest of the group will guess what it is.

Three insects get together. Take turns talking about yourselves and share your feelings.

FOR DISCUSSION

Describe your insect in the first person. For example "I am a bug. I am slippery. I slither along. People don't like me.", or whatever else comes to mind.

This description can also be done in writing, (depending on age). Each person, write a paragraph or short story, entitled, "I am a _____ (insect) ."

How do you think you would feel if you saw this insect in real life now? Any new insights into yourself? Can you share them with the group?

Sometimes in becoming the things we dislike we find out something about ourselves. It is now possible for energy that went into hating or fearing to be released for creative ways of being and thinking. The feared or disliked object loses its power over us, and understanding and compassion can take its place.

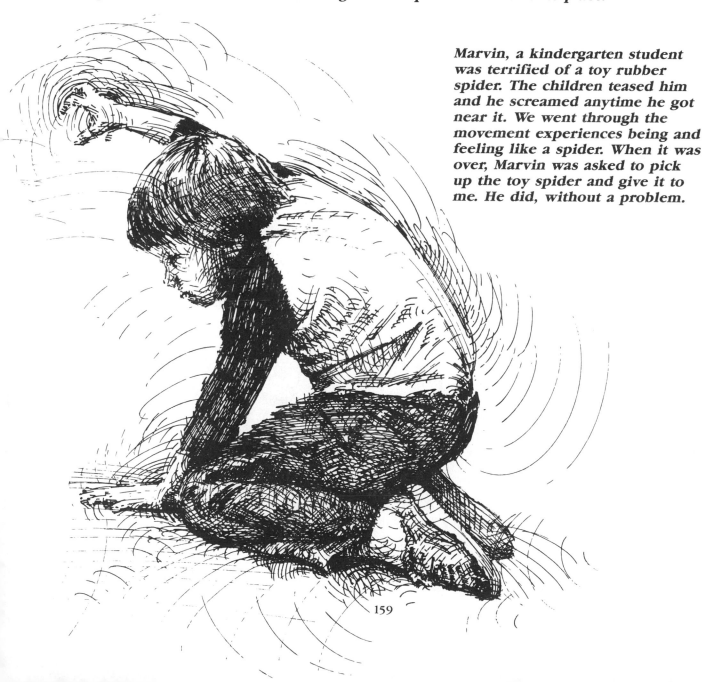

Marvin, a kindergarten student was terrified of a toy rubber spider. The children teased him and he screamed anytime he got near it. We went through the movement experiences being and feeling like a spider. When it was over, Marvin was asked to pick up the toy spider and give it to me. He did, without a problem.

YOUR ANIMAL

Sit or lie down in a comfortable position. Close your eyes. Take a deep breath and watch, in your mind's eye, the oxygen going through your entire body, clearing and cleaning as it goes through and out. Do this two more times, allowing the oxygen to flow to all organs of your body, purifying and relaxing.

Imagine a forest or a jungle. Listen to the sounds . . . Feel the warmth . . . See the foliage, the colors . . . Smell the greenery and see the animals near by.

You walk slowly through this forest, enjoying the colorful delights of the plants, wildflowers, and trees. You come to the edge of a clearing. You are hidden by the brush.

From across the clearing an animal moves into your sight. Notice how large or small it is, how it stands, how close to the ground or high up your animal is. Notice its colors . . . See its outer covering . . . Does it have thick skin? Fur? Feathers? Hard shell? How does it move?

This animal now moves back where it came from. Watch it go. You continue looking at the clearing from your hidden place. Another animal appears. **Repeat the same questions.**

The second animal will be the one we will work with.

Students will be more relaxed with the second visualization, and more likely relate to the second animal.

You are this animal. Feel its power or gentleness, its strength or grace. Feel all its qualities.

Choose three words to describe the qualities of your animal. Say to yourself
"I am a _____ _____ _____ (the 3 qualities) _____ (name of animal)."

Open your eyes, using soft focus, and move around the room as this animal . . . . You are the animal . . . . Be it . . . . Feel these qualities in your body. Feel it in your back, arms, legs, neck. Do you move tall and proud? Do you move close to the ground? Slowly? Quickly? How large are you? Feel this largeness. How small or dainty are you? Feel it!

Interact with other animals. Be sensitive to how they feel about you, and respond as your animal. Allow playfulness. Allow your encounter to reach a natural conclusion, and go on to another animal. How do you wish to be with your new playmate?

Now be yourself, with the qualities of your animal. Move around the room as yourself, feeling all the qualities of your animal in your entire body. Let your body bend, stretch, flow, turn. All parts are moving and feeling these qualities.

Be the animal again. Move as if you were the animal. Again feel the power or gentleness, massiveness or delicacy . . . . . Beautiful!

Allow this to go on for a while.

Now, be yourself again, feeling the qualities of your animal. Move luxuriously throughout the room as yourself, feeling these qualities.

Do you see someone with whom you would like to interact, while keeping the qualities of your animal? Have a conversation with sounds, not words . . . . Let the sounds express your feelings.

Come together in a group. Think again of the three words that would describe the qualities of your animal. Each person take a turn saying, "I am a _____ _____ _____ (the 3 qualities) _____ (name of animal)."

Are these the qualities you feel you have or would like to have?

MOVING TO INANIMATE OBJECTS

Choose any inanimate object, such as a pencil. We will move as a pencil.

"But a pencil doesn't move", you say. Well, let's discuss its qualities. Is it hard or soft?
Long . . .
    Pointed . . .
        Smooth . . .
            Straight . . .
                Inflexible . . .
                    Stiff . . .
                        Round?

We'll take three of these qualities into our body. Let's use long, smooth, and round. Create long, smooth, round movements all around the room. You don't have to look or shape yourself like a pencil to feel like it. Just feel its qualities in your body and use them in your movements. Feel them in your arms, fingers, back, everywhere. What other movements can you make? This is your pencil dance.

When we ask children to be a tree, we usually get a very static position. We therefore talk abut the qualities of the trunk or branches or leaves. And move with those qualities. We don't have to keep a tree shape. That would limit our movement.

Fantasy Environments, p. 157. will help stimulate the imagination for this movement activity.

CAST YOUR OWN CHARACTERS

Lie down on your back, legs extended and slightly apart. Arms loosely at your sides, eyes gently closed, and face relaxed. Take a deep breath, and hold it. As you let it out say the word "Relax" to yourself. Do this three times.

Visualize a comfortable room. You are there sitting in a corner, and cannot be seen. No one else is with you. Through a door your first character comes in.

What does she look like?

What is she wearing?

How does she act?

Observe this person for a while. ***Have 30 seconds of silence.***

Now she will leave the room by another door. Have three more characters enter the same way one at a time. Observe them as they come in and leave.

If you see a monster, don't be afraid. Give it something to eat. It might want to do something good for you, but doesn't know how yet. Help your monster. It will become your friend.

After your last person leaves, you may slowly open your eyes. In your own time, sit up and gather in groups of four.

Take turns acting out the different characters you imagined. Feel all their qualities in your body, one character at a time. Move with these qualities. Ask questions of each other and verbally share how you felt about each of your characters.

You may want to create a two or three minute play with your cast of characters. Really feel each one and own them. They are you.

Some of you may want to perform your play for the entire group.

USING THE SENSES

How does this piece
of chocolate smell?
''Sweet and thick?''
Move with those
qualities in your body.

Feel the sand
paper. What are
its qualities?
''Scratchy and
rough?'' Put them
into your body
and move to it.

Taste a lemon. How does it make your body
move? Let us see those qualities in your face
and all the way down to your fingertips and
toes.

Ring a triangle rhythm instrument. How does this sound make you want to move?

What other things can you taste, touch, feel, hear, or smell?

***To isolate the senses, it is better to close your eyes while you are tasting, feeling,
listening or smelling.***

PROPS

To have marvelous creative movement experiences you don't necessarily need to have a prop, just your own body. However, sometimes props are fun. They can stimulate other ideas, or be an extension of your body. They often help to lessen self-consciousness. Explore the following props in silence or add your favorite music.

KNIT FABRIC TUBES

HOW TO MAKE TUBES

Stretch material can sometimes be found in tubular shapes. If not, buy it flat, sew down the sides and keep the material open at both ends to create a tube. Cut it any length according to the size of the participants. If some tubes are twice as long as needed, more than one person can fit in at each end (feet first). It is also more exciting to have a variety of colors.

The children inside the material may create any body shape. Children outside may trace these shapes with their hands, deciding if they're straight or round.

Play inspirational music for participants to experiment with. Eventually ask that they partner up with someone else to form shapes. Some may watch. Improvisation within the material makes an incredible visual experience.

Environments for stories can be created by using some of the sculpting techniques in the previous chapters. Children can become worms or caterpillars, crawling through dirt, runners, or creating different wormlike shapes. Some of the children can create tunnel shapes for the worms to crawl through.

HOOPS

Let's just experiment with these hoops. Find all the possible things you can do with them. What shape are they? Keep on finding different things you can do. That's wonderful! Now try another way to use the hoops. Very good!

Add music to further stimulate the imagination. Often boys and girls will begin by trying things themselves, and then proceed to do something with a partner . . . Sometimes a leader will emerge, and organize a group activity.

Create a connecting sculpture. *See Levels, p. 102.*

Teachers can always have an organized activity afterward or the next day, but I prefer not to give them my ideas before they experiment with their own.

Put about 20 hoops on the floor. Everyone must walk only inside the hoops.

Call out a color, and everyone will end up in that color.

Children count how many are in each hoop. Which group has the most? The least?

Bring hoops over your head, under your knees, lie across, one foot inside, walk around, jump over, hop out backward, between your legs, next to you. Put your arm through, your head through, place the hoop on the floor. Lie inside and feel its roundness. Throw and catch them. Roll them. Put one body part inside, two body parts, three, four.

ADD YOUR OWN IDEAS!

THE CIRCLE LESSON

Think of something round. It's a line that goes around until it comes back to the same place. Can you make a circle with your fingers on one hand? Can you shape it larger using two hands? Can you shape a circle with your arms? Can you curl your whole body into a tight circle like a ball? Can you make a circle with your partner? Draw a circle with your finger on the floor.

Now jump into it. Tiptoe around the edge of your circle. Now sit in the middle of your circle. Let your feet walk around you touching the edge of your circle. Can you draw a circle in the air with your finger, elbow, nose? With what other part of your body can you draw a circle?

Everyone, join hands and form a circle. **Shape a circle using yarn around the children on the floor.** Skip, hop, walk, run around the outside of the yarn circle. Let's play some circle games. Draw a circle on someone's back.

Find all the things in the room shaped like a circle. Run your hands around them. Shape your body around them. Are there any parts of your body that are circular? Feel them. Head, eyes, tip of nose, elbows, knees.

Feel your body nice and soft and round . . . fingers, arms, back, everything round. Make a soft round circle dance. All body parts nice and round. Create your circle dance with a partner, in threes. Yes! They are beautiful.

SCARVES

Allow each student to choose a scarf from an assortment of many colors and shades.

What color do you feel like today? Are your scarves light or heavy? Throw them in the air. Do they come down quickly or slowly? Let your body move like the scarf, lightly and softly.

Let your arm move throughout the room creating patterns with your scarf. Allow your body to be an extension of your pattern by Bending . . .
>Swooping . . .
>>Twisting . . .
>>>Turning.

Really allow your whole body to feel the softness and lightness of the scarf. Feel the lightness in your Arms,
>Toes,
>>Neck,
>>>Back.

Be the lightness of the scarf. Be the scarf creating your own dance.
Your color. Your feelings.
Your body . . .
>Moving,
>>Bending,
>>>Twisting,
>>>>Stretching,
>>>>>Being,
>>>>>>Creating in space.

When you end your dance, throw your scarves into the air. Let them float gently to the ground. Allow your body to also float gently to the ground in the ending of your dance.

DIFFERENT SHADES OF PURPLE
How does purple make you feel? Angry . . .
>>>Regal . . .
>>>Passionate.
Move around the room with your purple scarves feeling the tension of anger in all parts of your body. Feel it in your Back . . .
>>Arms . . .
>>Neck . . .
>>Legs . . .
>>Everywhere.

"Angry movements" would be
Strong,
Swift,
Bristling,
Direct,
Vibrating,
Constrained.

Allow your body to experience these qualities.
Let your arms, legs, torso strike out in different directions,
and on different levels.

Be the Angry Purple!

Explore the other variations of purple in the same way.
Discuss the movement qualities of royal, passionate,
and whatever other feelings were mentioned by
participants. Then experience these qualities
in the body, and move it into space.

What does purple make you think of?
Grapes . . Velvet . . . Storms.

Describe the qualities of velvet.
Soft . . . Smooth . . . Deep.

Move softly and smoothly, feeling the depth
of each movement as you create your
purple-velvet dance throughout the space.

Face the person nearest you and
dance together, creating your
dance in response to each other
while still staying true to your
own uniqueness, a delicate
balance between individuality
and cooperation.

Create a final movement for
each other. Softly and
smoothly leave your
partner, dancing in a
different direction
and arrive at a new
place facing your
next partner.

Each new partner
will stimulate new
feelings, ideas, and
movements in you,
creating yet a
different dance
of purple-velvet.

173

Your Color

Look at all the scarves and choose the color you are feeling.

Choose a partner and share your feelings as to why you picked that color. Choose three words to describe the qualities of your color.

Say the qualities in the first person. "I am red. I am hot. I am fiery. I am excited."

Now move with these qualities in your body using the scarf.

Exchange with someone else's color and words, and dance with the new qualities and color. Be aware of what it's like to feel someone else's feelings. Exchange again.

Dance with your exchanged scarf, taking your turn in the center of the circle. Does the dance reflect the original owner's feelings?

DISCUSSION
How did you feel moving to other peoples feelings? Did you relate to any of them? Which one? Why?

Did you have difficulty expressing any of the colors?

Encourage different expressions for colors, realizing that we all have unique feelings and reactions, and that we also share these feelings. Any answer is correct. They come from the individual's own perceptions of how they see and feel color. The dance experience may come before or after verbal sharing. One may enhance the other.

Music and Color Shapes

Different musical instruments may have the qualities of different color shapes such as: the cello might have the rich deep brown shape. Flute . . . tall thin green. Violin . . . . yellow, reaching in all directions.

The same can be done with rhythm instruments. Cymbals may have the continuous resounding sound of purple. Drums may have a deep round black sound.

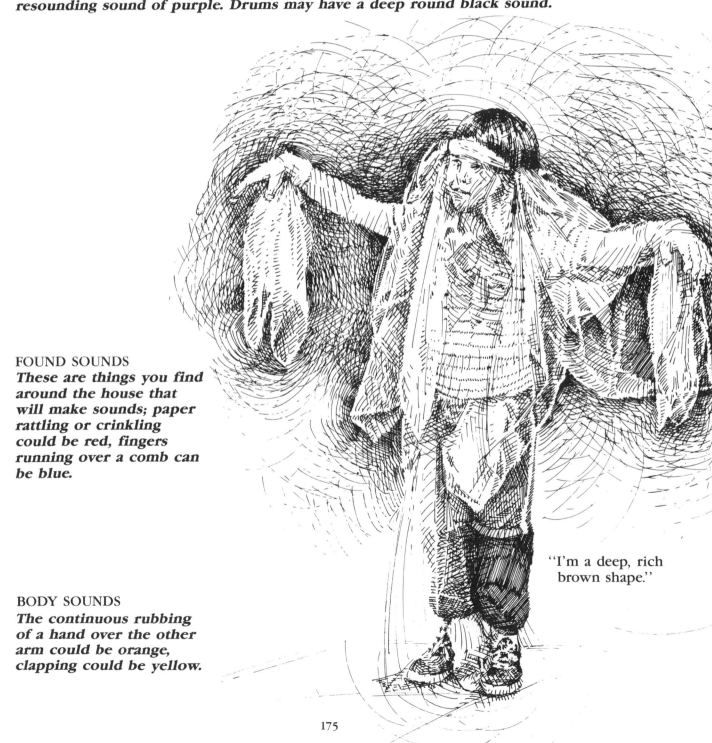

FOUND SOUNDS
These are things you find around the house that will make sounds; paper rattling or crinkling could be red, fingers running over a comb can be blue.

BODY SOUNDS
The continuous rubbing of a hand over the other arm could be orange, clapping could be yellow.

"I'm a deep, rich brown shape."

Happy Feelings

Let me see a happy face. How about happy hands? Can anyone show me happy feet? Add happy knees and legs. How about happy hips. Move your head and shoulders in a happy way.

Now add happy arms and hands. Your whole body looks happy! How do you feel?

Choose a happy colored scarf to do your happy dance.

Play upbeat happy music. Experiment with other feelings, brave, sad, angry, tired.

Mirror Feelings

See Mirroring for Awareness, p. 85. With a partner take turns expressing a feeling for your partner to mirror. Use facial expression. Allow the whole body to express the feeling. Begin with hands and slowly let the movements expand to the whole body. Continue to move throughout space. At a signal, change roles, and choose a different feeling.

QUESTIONS FOR DISCUSSION
What are some of the things that frighten you? That used to frighten you? Why is it sometimes good to be afraid? *Deep water, strange animals.* What is meant by mixed feelings? Can you feel two different ways about something at the same time? Why is it important to respect the feelings of others?

Feeling Folk Dance

Have two lines facing each other. The head couple will move down the center of the lines to the other end in a happy way. The people in lines will accompany with body or verbal sounds such as clapping, humming etc. The next couple will choose a different feeling to move down the lane. All will get a turn, and the rhythmic accompaniment will change appropriately.

Scarf Drama

Spontaneous dramatizations can be suggested by the scarves. The following ideas came from different movement workshops.

An instantaneous wedding party emerged with veils, wedding train, and flower petals (scarves) being thrown. A battle with swords . . . a celebration . . . a funeral . . . a bonfire . . . fall leaves . . . tunnels and caves. Many of these ideas take only a minute or two to re-enact. Others may be longer depending on age of participants and involvement in the idea.

VARIATIONS WITH SOUND
The participants can be divided. One half, use the colored scarves to carve shapes in space. Respond to the different sounds the other half of the group is creating.

or

The sounds may accompany the dancers as they respond to their different colors in movement.

The entire group may decide on an orchestration made up of body sounds, rhythm instruments, or found sounds. Combine the sounds in a repeatable way and then record them.

The group may then choreograph a dance to the orchestrated sounds. Add colors you feel are appropriate.

VERBAL SOUNDS
What sound would orange make? Laughing . . . light? *Participants can easily accompany themselves while creating their orange dance of feelings, things, shapes, and textures.*

Scarf Game With Partners

Using one scarf between two people, one throws it in the air for the other to catch before it reaches the ground. If thrown away from the partner, it will create a great deal of action. Add alternatives such as:

Can you catch it on your
                    Arm,
                       Finger,
                          Foot,
                             Elbow,
                                Head,
                                   Chest?
                    You add some.

Catching it with body parts can also be experienced with everyone having his own scarf.

This action game may be used as an introduction to the use of scarves for certain groups, such as older boys who may be resistant to using them.

FOR YOUNG CHILDREN
Using scarves or crepe paper streamers, attach two colors, one to each arm. Someone call out a color and you, children, will do an arm dance with that color.

Let your arm with the scarf lead you all over the room . . . . bending, swooping, twisting, and turning. Let the body follow all the movements of your scarf.

Fall Leaves

Using the idea of the wind, blow all the leaves forward, backward, sideways, up and down.

Call out fall colors one at a time.
All children with that color do a leaf dance. The others stay close to the floor, still moving your scarves.

Colors may be seasonal or used for holidays.

NEWSPAPER

All you need is a huge stack of newspapers, and possibly some masking tape.

You may do anything you want with this newspaper. Roll it,
Throw it,
Tear it,
Wear it,
Make objects,
Dress each other,
Skate on it,
Or whatever you can think of.

The only thing you may not do is read it or destroy projects of others.

The first time you do this experience with young children, they usually get into a lot of tearing or throwing and very few usable ideas. The second time, it is a good idea to add more structure by saying that something must be created out of the process, such as a costume or a prop.

Begin working by yourself. Eventually you may interact. Play with each other, possibly using each other's props. Help each other create costumes, or instant drama with what you've made.

Please respect whether or not someone may want to interact with you, and appreciate each other's work.

Any instrumental music with a variety of moods will be good for background. Soundtracks from films are usually very good. This could go on for a half hour to an hour, depending upon the size of the group and intensity of involvement.

A variation, but expensive, is to use very large sheets of colored tissue paper. Newsprint can also be used. These last two will not be as dirty as newspaper.

Cleanup at the end can also be a fun activity. Put cheerful music on. Have about four large trash bags available, and the whole group will have the messiest room clean in five minutes, while enjoying doing it.

ROPES

Clothesline will do, each, three to four feet long.

Create designs on the floor that you will follow with your whole body.

Recreate the same design in the air.

Use the entire space in the room to remake your design without the rope.

Alternate sitting and lying down, holding both ends of the rope in your hands. Stretch your foot or both your feet into the middle. Stretch and bend your legs creating different shapes with the rope.

Bring your arms over your head, behind you.

Take your legs up, to the side and down. Allow your body to turn to the side, roll, sit, lie down.

Each movement stretches the rope into a different shape.

Connect with two others, one at each end, and one in the middle of the rope. In slow motion pulling, create an improvisation moving on all levels.

Do this in groups of four, then eight, and so on, until the whole class is working together.

Create a constellation of stars.

Individually use the rope for going
>> Under,
>>> Over,
>>>> Around you,
>>>>> Next to you
>>>>>> Or between your legs.

Make a circle with the rope and jump in and out of it,
>>> Lie across it,
>>> Step on it.
Make letters, shapes or numbers with your rope. Place one, two, or three body parts inside your shape.

Hold both ends in one of your hands. Swing it in front,
>>> In back
>>>> And to the side of you making patterns in the air.
Make sure you have plenty of room around you. Dance with your rope, and be it.

Have a dialogue with your prop.

183

SHADOW PLAY

Use a lamp or overhead projector for a light source. Experiment, one at a time, creating any kind of shadow shapes you want. In small groups you can make some connecting shadow sculptures. ***You may use themes such as, softness, being scared, geometric shapes, letters, or even just feet or hands.***

Place some block letters, numbers, or shapes on the projector. Trace their shadows with a pointer. Try to shape your own shadow around them.

Use slides of places you are learning about.
Place your shadow in the pictures. Have your shadow walk down a street, sit on a chair, relate to a person, swim in a body of water, go down a waterfall, up the mountain or dance in an elegant ballroom. What other environments can you think of?

Take turns moving in and out of these environments creating the appropriate poses and sculptures.

Try slides of art forms.
Let your shadow move through the picture as the art form inspires you to do.

Project slides of animals. Music can be added for background effect.
Move through the image as that animal would move.

This was one of my most memorable classes with Dr. Sarah Chapman in Dance Experiences for Children at Temple University.

COLOR
With the use of different colored gels you can create color environments. Project red, yellow, blue, etc. on different walls and let your shadow move as the different colors affect you. See Different Shades of Purple, p. 172.

On a sunny day go outside and play with creating your own shadows.

OTHER PROPS

Gloves, hats, capes, sashes, long skirts, parachutes, balloons, streamers, balls, soap bubbles, masks, bamboo poles, confetti, any found object and whatever else you can think of.

CONCLUSION

*The individual is the center of A MOVING EXPERIENCE.
Each person will gain something unique, central
to her own being. And the Moving Experience
moves on through you and your ongoing
interpretation, integration and
implementation of its
contents.*

185

CELEBRATE THE COMING OF FALL

A WORKSHOP FOR ADULTS

By combining experiences in this book you can create a workshop with a theme for many different populations. Following is an example of a two hour workshop, presented to the members of the Association for Humanistic Psychology, September, 1984. It is based on activities done with elementary-aged children. The intent and language were changed to meet the needs of the presenter and the population.

Some of these movement experiences may seem very simple. What we are feeling, thinking, or visualizing as we go through them is what makes them powerful and meaningful. The dialogue which runs throughout is intended to inspire positive change and to empower the participants with their possibilities.

Most groups are not familiar with each other, so these movement experiences are structured to help get acquainted. We begin with ourselves, then connect with a partner, and then larger and larger groups till we are relating to everyone. The structure of the experiences gives a certain amount of safety, building up to the end where there is totally free movement.

THE WORKSHOP BEGINS

CHANGES (Introduction)
We are all in a season of change, "Autumn" . . . . The leaves are changing colors and falling away leaving the branches bare. We too are changing. We have to let go of the old and make way for the new. We have to let go of ideas, feelings, and ways of being that are no longer working for us, and make way for new growth and more appropriate behaviors.

VISUALIZATION
Please get into a relaxed position. Close your eyes. See yourself in your mind's eye . . . .
                    What are you wearing?
                    What is your position?
                    Are you sitting or standing?
                        Notice your hair, your expression. This is about changes.
See yourself doing something you always wanted to do and haven't done yet . . .
A new vision . . .
    A loving vision . . . .
      A new priority . . .
        Possibly a new friendship.

Be brave, let yourself envision something you really want, something that will make you feel marvelous. In silence, take a few moments to enjoy your newly created vision.

Soon I will count to six. At that moment you will be able to open your eyes feeling completely refreshed . . . 1 . . . 2 . . . You are beginning to come back to this room in this time and place . . . 3 . . . 4 . . . Maybe you need to stretch a little . . . legs, arms, back . . . Yes, do let your body stretch . . . 5 . . . 6 . . . Open your eyes feeling refreshed and happy and energized, feeling better than you ever felt before.

OPENING
Please choose a partner . . . . One of you curl up tightly in a ball. Your partner will very slowly, very gently open you up until you are totally uncurled and stretched out in perfect alignment. Make sure your partner's body is always supported either by you or by the floor. The partner being uncurled should not have to put any effort into this. He just needs to be open to it . . . . You will be open and stretched out to your new vision of yourself . . . to your new possibilities . . . . You will be like a beautiful flower being opened to the sun . . . a new healing sun . . . It will be as if you are a baby opening up to a new world.

Before changing roles with your partner, allow yourself to feel totally open, not moving for a few moments. When both partners have experienced the opening, you may verbally share your feelings with each other.

PASSIVE-ACTIVE

Join another set of two and become a group of four. Each one in your group of four will take a turn at creating your new vision of how you would like to be in the world. Sculpt the other three people in your group. Shape them as if they were clay, into positions that they will be able to hold. Let them become your environment. They could be other people or objects . . . trees . . . water . . . rocks . . . animals . . . . anything you want.

When you have your new environment sculpted just the way you would like, join it and become part of this new vision of yours . . .

Create your fantasy . . .

Create your new world . . .

You may try different shapes or ideas before you are satisfied with the new sculpted environment that you will be part of.

Take your time.

Enjoy the process.

This is your moment . . . .

You may verbally share your creation with your group. Someone else in the group may take a turn and repeat the process until all four have had a turn.

NEGATIVE-POSITIVE SPACES

Now join another group of four and become a group of eight. If we are making changes in our lives we will see new shapes . . . new forms. It may feel like the shedding of old skins. Half of you create a sculpture. Do this by creating a sculpture you can hold, and at the same time be attached to one or two of your partners on different levels with different body parts. For example, shoulder to hip, foot to hand. Also make sure there are lots of empty spaces between you, so make your sculpture as large as possible . . . . The spaces are made for the positive new things,

New thoughts,

New ideas to enter . . . .

The other half of your group slowly walk around the sculpture seeing the new shapes and also the shapes created by the empty or negative spaces.

Which space attracts you? . . . .

Put your body into it, fill up the empty spaces . . .

Shape yourself into the new world that was created for you.

What forms are you in? . . . .

What shape does your body take? . . . .

What space appealed to you?

The first half of the group, in slow motion, very carefully leave the sculpture so as not to disturb what was created by the second group . . . . Be flexible . . . . Let go of your shape. You will come back in yet another way . . . . Walk around, see the new sculpture . . . . and the new spaces.

What appeals to you? In slow motion re-enter this new world. Try out this new environment . . . Find new ways of fitting your body into these newly created shapes. Changing and rechanging, creating and recreating . . . . Like leaves falling away colorfully, making way for new creations.

The second group, again in slow motion, leaves the environment, leaving the newly formed shapes. This is an ongoing process of leaving the known, taking a risk, looking at the new and entering it in a new way, constantly reshaping your body, finding new ways to fit into the world. ***Repeat about ten times as long as interest allows, or for the length of the musical piece.***

FREE FLOW
To create a new relationship with life . . . with people . . . dolphins . . . trees . . . animals . . . insects . . . flowers . . . blades of grass . . . we will flow in and out of the shapes formed by others as they are simultaneously moving in and out of the created space . . . A continuous flowing of the ever-changing shaping of our bodies.

Getting to as many people as possible . . .
   Blending and fusing . . .
      Coupling and individuating . . . We are trees . . .
            We are air . . .
              We are insects . . .
                We are the dolphins . . .
               We are everything . . .
     We are all in the same family of living things and living beings.

SCARVES
Coming into the new. ***While the following is spoken, light colorful scarves are being pulled out of a bag and thrown into the air, being caught by the participants. . . .*** Possibly to new jobs or to new relationships, or old ones with new freshness and renewed intimacy.

New ideas . . . . New love . . . . ***Participants have been dancing with the scarves. Some dressing up in them, tucking them into their clothes, or putting them on their heads, necks and wrists. They are throwing them into the air and catching them with different body parts. They are throwing scarves to each other, communicating through dance and free movement. There is an increased excitement, high energy, and a general letting go.***

Nature is with us, also about to burst with brilliant colors . . .
Passionate colors . . .
A new season . . .
A shedding . . .
A getting ready season .

And we too are shedding . . .
Shedding old skins . . .
Trying on new ones .

Feel your colors. . .
Blend with others in this space with you . . .
Feel the power of change . . .
Of your brilliance . . .
Of the freshness of beginning.

Shed your judgments . . .
Open to your hearts . . .
Shed your labels . . .
Open to renewed beauty . . .
Shed your unnecessary baggage . . .
Open to love.

This is a time for harvesting . . .
Of gathering in the fruits of your labor . . .
Gather to yourself . . .
Take from the sky . . .
From the earth . . .
From each other . . .
Gently . . . lovingly . . .
Take . . . receive .

You worked for it . . .
You deserve everything . . .
Feel the excitement of receiving the fruits of your labor . . .
Gather it in . . .
Feel full . . .
Feel rich . . .
Feel plentiful.

You ARE full . . .
You ARE prosperous . . .
Feel the tingliness of your skin . . .
Feel the excitement of having.

Share your riches . . .

Celebrate yourselves . . .

Regenerate . . .

Be free . . .

BE.

SUGGESTED READINGS

The following are books I have enjoyed over the years while developing my movement and awareness program. Some have provided specific movement education ideas and experiences while others have inspired and probed my own imagination helping me to offer an expanding, creative environment for others.

Bagley, Michael, and Hess, Karen
200 Ways Of Using Imagery In The Classroom
Trillium Press, NY
A guide for developing imagination and creativity in elementary students while learning all areas of the curriculum.

Barlin, Anne and Robbin, Tamara
Move And Be Moved
Learning Through Movement, 5757 Ranchito, Van Nuys, CA 91401
Dance education and therapy with beautiful illustrations and sensitive movement suggestions.

Berkus, Rusty
Appearances, Clearings Through The Masks Of Our Existence
Red Rose Press, Encino, CA
About self acceptance. Simple poetry, magically illustrated.

Bessell, Harold, Ph. D. and Palomares, Uvaldo, Ed.D.
Human Development Program
Human Development Training Institute, Inc., 1081 E. Main St., El Cajon, CA 92021
Different activity guides for each grade, pre-school through sixth grade. Wonderful daily experiences to do throughout the year to help children feel good about themselves and each other.

Canfield, Jack and Wells, Harold
100 Ways To Enhance Self Concept In The Classroom.
Prentice-Hall, Inc., Englewood Cliffs, NJ
A wealth of experiences for children and adults in school or home in enhancing self concept.

Canner, Norma
And A Time To Dance
Beacon Press, Boston, MA
An inspiring pictorial essay of movement therapy with retarded children.

Carr, Rachel
Be A Frog, A Bird Or A Tree, Creative Yoga Exercises for Children
Harper and Row, NY
Delightfully illustrated and photographed. Easy to learn yoga positions for children.

Chapman, Sarah Ed.D.
Movement Education In The United States
Movement Education Publications, Philadelphia, PA 19114
Background of the development of movement education and its emergence in the United States from 1900-1960.

Cherry, Clare
Creative Movement For The Developing Child
Lear Siegler, Inc., Fearon Publishers, Belmont, CA
Lots of movement songs with helpful movement suggestions for the three to five year old.

Clark, Barbara
Optimizing Learning: The Integrative Education Model In The Classroom
Merrill Publishing Co., Columbus, OH
The author of **Growing Up Gifted** translates the latest technical and scientific findings into easy-to-understand procedures for the brain-compatible classroom.

Complo, Sister Jannita Marie
Dramakinetics In The Classroom
Plays, Inc., Boston, MA
Many stimulating and simple ideas to use for creative dramatics and improvised movement.

Curtiss, Deborah
Introduction To Visual Literacy, A Guide to the Visual Arts and Communication
Prentice-Hall, Inc., Englewood Cliffs, NJ
Illuminates the process of visual communication for creator and receiver alike. Designed for all persons who have an interest in their visual perceptions and wish to know and see more.

Davon, Ashoh, forward by Pearl Buck
The Kiss
The Theosophical Publishing House, Wheaton, IL
A charming story about cooperation, written for children and the child within.

Dimondstein, Geraldine
Children Dance In The Classroom
Macmillan Publishing Co. Inc., NY
Well organized and easy to use. Many good examples of movement experiences.

Duncan, Isadora
My Life
Liveright Publishing Corp., NY
An extraordinary story about an amazing woman who did her own thing in dance. Her life and dance style inspires the idea of being free and being yourself.

Fleming, Gladys Andrews, editor
Children's Dance
American Alliance for Health, Physical Education and Recreation, 1201 16th St. NW, Washington, DC 20036
A compilation of the good ideas of many dance educators using creative movement with children.

Fluegelman, Andrew
New Games
More New Games
Doubleday and Co., NY
Two books offering a wonderful assortment of fun, non-competitive sports for all ages. Requires from two to an unlimited number of participants.

Frank, Frederick
The Zen Of Seeing
Random House, NY
This very special book of learning to draw without trying to make 'art' can be a helpful reminder that we all have the creative spark.

Fuller, Rebecca and Syons, Nancy
Openings And Inner Workings
The Footprint Press, Sonoma, CA
A collection of simple experiments designed to give openings into ways of perceiving oneself as a mover in a world of motion. The drawings and poems lead into the inner dances in the dimensions of time and space.

Furth, Hans, G.
Piaget For Teachers
Prentice-Hall, Englewood Cliffs, NJ
The educational implications of Piaget's theory.

Gilbert, Ann Green
Teaching The Three R's Through Movement Experiences
Burgess Publishing Co., Minneapolis, MN
Specific movement ideas for curriculum areas.

Gilliom, Bonnie
Basic Movement Education For Children
Addison-Wesley Publishing Co., Reading, MA
Many activities to introduce movement and creativity into a physical education program.

Hamblin, Kay
Mime, A Playbook Of Silent Fantasy
Doubleday and Co., Garden City, NY
Beautifully photographed book helps all ages to use mime. Easy to follow and fun to explore warm ups, exercises, games and routines.

Hanna, Thomas
Bodies In Revolt: A Primer In Somatic Thinking
Holt, Rinehart & Winston, Inc., NY
A stimulating discussion and synthesis of the work of such brilliant thinkers as Darwin, Freud, Lorenz, Piaget, Reich, Kant, Kierkegaard, Marx, Cassirer, Camus, Merleau-Ponty and Nietzsche.

H'Doubler, Margaret
Dance, A Creative Art Experience
University of Wisconsin Press, Madison, WI
A warm philosophical statement concerning the value of dance in education and in life.

Houston, Jean
The Possible Human
J. P. Tarcher, Inc., Los Angeles, CA
A course in enhancing physical, mental, and creative abilities. Shows how you can see more, hear more, remember more, and draw on more of your inner resources.

Jennings, Sue, editor
Creative Therapy
Pitman Publishing, NY
Ways of fostering and developing creativity expressed in different ways.

Laban, Rudolf, revised by Lisa Ullmann
Modern Educational Dance
Plays, Inc., Boston, MA
A guide for teachers and parents. Gives the essentials of a free dance technique and the principles of movement observation. Also describes 16 themes suitable for different age groups.

Lehane, Stephen
The Creative Child
Prentice-Hall, Inc., Englewood Cliffs, NJ
How to encourage the natural creativity of your preschooler. 'The youngster from two to six isn't waiting for something to happen, he or she already engages in the most creative part of life.'

Madeja, Stanley
All The Arts For Every Child
Final report on the Arts in General Education project in the school district of University City, MO
Copies from the JDR 3rd Fund, Inc. 50 Rockefeller Plaza, NY 10020
Interesting projects in the arts, beautifully photographed.

Mettler, Barbara
Materials Of Dance As A Creative Art Activity
Mettler Studios, 3131 N. Cherry Ave., Tucson, AZ 85719
This book is very useful and well organized with plenty of good ideas. It is written in an easy workshop format.

Michaelis, Bill and Dolores
Learning Through Non-Competitive Activities And Play
Learning Handbooks, Palo Alto, CA
Imaginative movement projects and games that involve children in cooperative learning.

Orlick, Terry
The Cooperative Sports And Games Book
Pantheon Books, NY
An absolutely delightful book with lots of creative fun games for all ages that challenges without competition.

Paulus, Trina
Hope For The Flowers
Paulist Press, Paramus, NJ
A tale partly about life, partly about revolution and lots about hope for adults and others (including caterpillars who can read).

Pica, Rae
Poetry In Motion
Front Row Experience, 540 Discovery Bay Blvd., Byron, CA 94514
Poems and activities for moving and learning with young children.

Rogers, Carl
On Becoming A Person
Houghton Mifflin Co., Boston, MA
One of the world's most distinguished psychologists speaks of his views on human personality and growth.

Rowan, Betty
Learning Through Movement
Teachers College Press, Columbia University, NY
Integrating movement into the curriculum, delightfully written by a teacher of school children and dance.

Scheflen, Albert, M.D.
Body Language And Social Order
Prentice-Hall, Inc., Englewood Cliffs, NJ
A fascinating look at how we control and communicate non-verbally.

Schoop, Trudi
Won't You Join The Dance: A Dancer's Essay Into The Treatment Of Psychosis
National Press, Palo Alto, CA
A sensitive and personal account of the successes and failures of a pioneer dance therapist.

Segal, Edith
Be My Friend
Come With Me
Edith Segal, 60 Plaza Street, Apt. 3A, Brooklyn, NY 11238
Two books of poems that were very special to my kindergarten children.

Stevens, John O.
Awareness: Exploring, Experimenting, Experiencing
Real People Press, Moab, UT
More than 100 experiments expanding the awareness of yourself, your surroundings, and your interaction with others. Based on the Gestalt therapy of Dr. Fritz Perls.

Torbert, Marianne
Follow Me
The Leonard Gordon Institute for Human Development Through Play,
c/o Marianne Torbert, Ph.D., Temple University, Philadelphia, PA 19122
Movement activities for children that encourage social growth, self control, listening, and fun.

Warner, Sylvia Ashton
Teacher
Bantam Books, NY
The story of an amazing woman and her inspiring method of teaching based on joy and love.

Wiener, Jack and Lidstone, John
Creative Movement For Children
Von Nostrand Reinhold Co., NY
More than 300 excellent photographs showing elementary aged children using different locomotive movements with flow, time, and space.

Witkin, Kate
To Move, To Learn
Temple University Press, Philadelphia, PA
Personal heart warming stories of children with difficult physical and mental problems who learn to participate in, and love creative movement, and themselves.

My Favorite Songs

The children in my kindergarten class sang **The Greatest Love of All** every day along with **The National Anthem**. We called it **The Children's National Anthem.**

> "I believe the children
> are our future
> Teach them well and let them
> lead the way."

artist, George Benson
from WEEKEND IN L.A.

Below are more songs the children were inspired by and loved to sing. (I also include all the Hap Palmer records by Educational Activities.)

We Are The World
We Are The Children

from WE ARE THE WORLD

Listen, Listen, Listen
To My Heart's Song
        and
From Thee I Receive
To Thee I Give

artist, Robbie Gass
from ON WINGS OF SONG
Spring Hill
Many Blessings
Box 124
Ashby, MA 01431

It's in every one of us
    to be wise
Find your heart
    open up both your eyes.

artist, David Pomerantz
from IT'S IN EVERY ONE OF US
Arista Records, Inc.

Let's Be Friends
        and
All About Me

artist, Miss Jackie
Gryphon House
Mt. Ranier, MD

MUSICAL SELECTIONS

The following list is music that I have found to be effective at enhancing the experiences described in this book. I chose music that inspires me, knowing that the participants will respond to my excitement and positive energy, for enthusiasm is contagious. My selections come from a variety of sources including the classics, as well as sound tracks from film, modern and New Age music. I usually do not use popular tunes of the day in order to avoid predictable stylized responses. Rather, I try to encourage each individual to find his own unique form of movement. My list grows every time I listen to a melody or rhythm that I feel inspires creative movement. It is important for leaders of these movement explorations to add their own personal music selections so that children will be inspired by their enthusiasm.

The suggested music is listed in two ways. Part A gives the music selection and several suitable movement experiences with the page number where each activity can be found. Part B reverses the information, giving the movement experiences first, followed by a number of musical options. Album titles are CAPITALIZED, followed by individual musical selections in *italics*. Most of these music pieces can be found in your local music store. Some may be found in what are known as New Age book and record shops.

MUSIC SUGGESTIONS PART A

Classical

Chopin, *Nocturne, B-Flat Minor, Opus 9 No. 1*
        Dance of Number Nine, 34
        Back to Back, 82
        Murals, Spring, 140
        The Circle Lesson, 171

Chopin, *Les Sylphides*
        Open-Close, 5
        The Letter Dance, 64
        Mirroring, 84
        Using Yarn, 129
        Weaving, 134
        Knit Fabric Tubes, 169
        The Circle Lesson, 171

Haydn, *Flute Quartet, Opus 5*
        Exaggerate the Movement, 97
        Shadow Play, 184

HOOKED ON CLASSICS, Louis Clark conducting The Royal Philharmonic Orchestra
        Opposites, 7
        Feet Patterns, 141
        Hoops, 170
        Scarves, 172-179
        Newspaper, 180

Satie, *Gymnopedies*
> Feeling Shapes, 68
> Giving Gifts, 81
> Gentle Sway, 98
> Flowing Healing Sculpting, 113

Strauss, J., *The Blue Danube*
> Mirroring, 84
> Lines and Drawing, 129
> Balance, 132
> Murals, Spring, 140
> Dances From Different Lands: Vienna, 148
> Scarves, 172, 177

Tchaikovsky, *Sleeping Beauty: Panorama*
> Right and Left: Dancing It, 51
> Magnets, 86
> Using Yarn, 129

Tchaikovsky, *The Nutcracker Suite: Pas de Deux*
> Mirroring, 84
> Magnets, 86
> Levels, 102
> Music Qualities, slow, light, sustained, 147

Tchaikovsky, *Swan Lake*
> Space Flow, 23
> The Letter Dance, 64
> Levels, 102
> Lines and Drawing, 129

Wagner, *Die Walküre: Ride of The Valkyries*
> Feelings, anger, 10, 173, 176
> Words with a Theme: Flames, 78

Below are some albums that I use to enhance the improvisation that often develops spontaneously from the movement. Some of the above music is included in these albums.

FIREWORKS with Eugene Ormandy
> Khatchaturian, *Sabre Dance*
> Wagner, *The Ride of The Valkyries*
> Rimsky-Korsakov, *The Dance of The Tumblers*
> Saint-Saëns, *Samson and Delilah*
>> and many more.

THE SORCERER'S APPRENTICE with Leonard Bernstein
> Mussorgsky, *Night On Bald Mountain*
> Saint-Saëns, *Danse Macabre*

THE FANTASY FILM WORLD OF BERNARD HERRMANN
> *Journey To The Center Of The Earth*
> *The Seventh Voyage Of Sinbad*
> *The Day The Earth Stood Still*

LULLABY FROM THE WOMB, Dr. Hajime Murooda
> Massenet, *Thais: Meditation*
> Mascagni, *Cavalleria Rusticana: Intermezzo*
> Saint-Saëns, *Carnival Of Animals: The Swan*
> Tchaikovsky, *Sleeping Beauty: Panorama*

SCORES FROM FILMS AND BROADWAY SHOWS

SINGERS AND GROUPS

NEW AGE

MUSIC SUGGESTIONS PART B

7   Opposites
        FORBIDDEN OVERTURES (See listing on p. 203 to order)
        HOOKED ON CLASSICS
        MODERN TUNES FOR RHYTHMS AND INSTRUMENTS, Hap Palmer
        ROCKY III, *Eye Of The Tiger*
        SNOWFLAKES ARE DANCING, Tomita
        THE STING

10   Body Awareness and Feelings
        Happy: HOTTER THAN JULY: *Happy Birthday,* Stevie Wonder
        Sad: JONATHAN LIVINGSTON SEAGULL
        Angry: Wagner, *Die Walküre: Ride Of The Valkyries*
        Angry: DRUMS OF PASSION, Olatunji
        Tired: MOTHER EARTH'S LULLABY, Synchestra
        Brave: Rimsky-Korsakov, *Scheherazade: The Sea And The Boat of Sinbad*

11   Opening
        THE FAIRY RING, Mike Rowland
        JONATHON LIVINGSTON SEAGULL
        THE LEGEND OF THE ROSE: *The Rose,* Winafred Lucas
        Massenet, *Thais: Meditation*
        Pachelbel, *Canon In D*

15   Exploring Space
        ANTARCTICA
        MOTHER EARTH'S LULlABY, Synchestra
        PETALS, Bernoff and Allen
        SILK ROAD SUITE, Kitaro

22   Personal Space Stretch Dance
        ANTARCTICA
        CATS: *Memory*
        Mozart, *Concerto No. 21 In C Major For Piano And Orchestra: Andante*
          (theme from ELVIRA MADIGAN)

23   Space Flow
        CAT STEVENS' GREATEST HITS: *Morning Has Broken*
        FLASH DANCE, *Love Theme*
        SNOWFLAKES ARE DANCING, Tomita
        SOUNDS OF SILENCE: *Sounds Of Silence,* Simon and Garfunkel
        Saint-Saëns, *Carnival Of Animals: The Swan*
        Tchaikovsky, *Swan Lake*

28   Measuring Space
        MODERN TUNES FOR RHYTHMS AND INSTRUMENTS, Hap Palmer

31   Moving to Number Four
        TRANS-EUROPE EXPRESS: *Trans-Europe Express,* Kraftwerk

34   Dance of Number Nine
        ANTARCTICA
        CAVERNA MAGICA, Andreas Vollenweider
        FORBIDDEN OVERTURES (See listing on p. 203 to order)
        MODERN TUNES FOR RHYTHMS AND INSTRUMENTS, Hap Palmer
        STAR WARS
        Chopin, *Nocturne, B-Flat Minor, Opus 9 No. 1*

35   Passing a Ball
        FORBIDDEN OVERTURES (See listing on p. 203 to order)
        THE STING
        TRANS-EUROPE EXPRESS: *Trans-Europe Express,* Kraftwerk

95   Rubber Bands
        AFRO CLASSICS: *Theme From Love Story,* Hubert Laws
        CAT STEVENS' GREATEST HITS: *Morning Has Broken*
        CAVERNA MAGICA, Andreas Vollenweider
        FIRST TAKE: *Angelitos Negros,* Roberta Flack
        A RAINBOW PATH, Kay Gardner
        SNOWFLAKES ARE DANCING, Tomita
        Mascagni, *Cavalleria Rusticana: Intermezzo*

96   The Triangle
        AFRO CLASSICS: *Theme From Love Story,* Hubert Laws
        CATS: *Memory*
        DANCEPIECES: *In the Upper Room,* Philip Glass
        FORBIDDEN OVERTURES (See listing on p. 203 to order)
        MAN OF LA MANCHA
        STAR WARS

97   Exaggerate the Movement
        CAVERNA MAGICA, Andreas Vollenweider
        JOURNEY THROUGH THE SECRET LIFE OF PLANTS: *Ecclesiastes,* Stevie Wonder
        Haydn, *Flute Quartet, Opus 5*
        Ravel, *Bolero*

98   Gentle Sway
        THE FAIRY RING, Mike Rowland
        THE LEGEND OF THE ROSE: *The Rose,* Winafred Lucas
        MOTHER EARTH'S LULLABY, Synchestra
        PETALS, Bernoff and Allen
        Massenet, *Thais: Meditation*
        Pachelbel, *Canon In D*
        Satie, *Gymnopedies*

102   Levels
        AFRO CLASSICS: *Theme From Love Story,* Hubert Laws
        AUTUMN and/or DECEMBER, George Winston
        CATS: *Memory*
        Mascagni, *Cavalleria Rusticana: Intermezzo*
        Tchaikovsky, *The Nutcracker Suite, Pas de Deux*
        Tchaikovsky, *Swan Lake*

105   Reach Out and Touch
        DIANA ROSS' GREATEST HITS: *Reach Out And Touch*
        HOTTER THAN JULY: *Happy Birthday,* Stevie Wonder

109   Body Impulse
        CHARIOTS OF FIRE
        DANCEPIECES: *In the Upper Room,* Philip Glass

110   Passive-Active
        ANTARCTICA
        KOSMOS, Tomita
        MAN OF LA MANCHA
        STAR WARS
        THE STING

113   Flowing Healing Sculpting
           THE FAIRY RING, Mike Rowland
           JONATHAN LIVINGSTON SEAGULL
           MOTHER EARTH'S LULLABY, Synchestra
           PETALS, Bernoff and Allen
           A RAINBOW PATH, Kay Gardner
           Massenet, *Thais: Meditation*
           Pachelbel, *Canon In D*
           Satie, *Gymnopedies*

118   Creating Environments, city
           FLASH DANCE: *What A Feeling*
           THE STING

120   Other Environments
           A circus: Saint-Saëns, *Danse Macabre*
           A supermarket: Saint-Saëns, *Samson And Delilah: Bacchanale*
           The zoo: STAR WARS
           Our planetary system: JOURNEY TO THE CENTER OF THE EARTH
           The desert: A RAINBOW PATH, Kay Gardner
           Jail: TRANSFER STATION BLUE, Michael Shrieve
           A jungle: FORBIDDEN OVERTURES (See p. 203 to order)

127   String Painting with Levels
           AUTUMN and/or DECEMBER, George Winston
           THE BEST OF JUDY COLLINS: *Suzanne*
           CATS: *Memory*
           YEARNING AND HARMONY, Tri Atma with Klaus Netzle
           Saint-Saëns, *Carnival Of Animals: The Swan*

128   Body Parts Collage
           FLASH DANCE
           ROCKY III: *Eye Of The Tiger*
           TRANSFER STATION BLUE, Michael Shrieve

129   Lines and Drawing
           AUTUMN and/or DECEMBER, George Winston
           FIRST TAKE: *Angelitos Negros,* Roberta Flack
           FLASH DANCE
           KOSMOS, Tomita
           MOVIN', Hap Palmer
           SILK ROAD SUITE, Kitaro
           Strauss, J., *The Blue Danube*
           Tchaikovsky, *Sleeping Beauty: Panorama*
           Tchaikovsky, *Swan Lake*

129   Using Yarn
           AUTUMN and/or DECEMBER, George Winston
           CHARIOTS OF FIRE
           Chopin, *Les Sylphides*
           Mozart, *Concerto No. 21 In C Major For Piano And Orchestra: Andante*
               (theme from ELVIRA MADIGAN)
           Ravel, *Bolero*
           Saint-Saëns, *Carnival Of Animals: The Swan*

130   Negative and Positive Spaces
           CHARIOTS OF FIRE
           DANCEPIECES: *In the Upper Room,* Philip Glass
           THE FAIRY RING, Mike Rowland
           SILK ROAD SUITE, Kitaro
           SNOWFLAKES ARE DANCING, Tomita

209

170   Hoops

                  HOOKED ON CLASSICS
                  JOURNEY TO THE CENTER OF THE EARTH
                  MODERN TUNES FOR RHYTHMS AND INSTRUMENTS, Hap Palmer
                  MOVIN', Hap Palmer
                  STAR WARS
                  TRANSFER STATION BLUE, Michael Shrieve
                  Saint-Saëns, *Samson And Delilah: Bacchanale*

171   The Circle Lesson

                  CATS: *Memory*
                  CAT STEVENS' GREATEST HITS: *Morning Has Broken*
                  Chopin, *Les Sylphides*
                  Chopin, *Nocturne, B-Flat Minor, Opus 9 No. 1*
                  Mozart, *Concerto No. 21 In C Major For Piano And Orchestra: Andante*
                      (theme from ELVIRA MADIGAN)
                  Ravel, *Bolero*

172   Scarves
177   Scarf Drama

                  CATS: *Memory*
                  HOOKED ON CLASSICS
                  MOTHER EARTH'S LULLABY, Synchestra
                  THE LEGEND OF THE ROSE, *The Rose,* Winafred Lucas
                  Chopin, *Nocturne, B-flat Minor, Opus 9, No. 1*
                  Mozart, *Concerto No. 21 In C Major For Piano And Orchestra: Andante*
                        (theme from ELVIRA MADIGAN)
                  Strauss, J., *The Blue Danube*

172   Scarves: Different Shades of Purple

                  FIRST TAKE: *Angelitos Negros,* Roberta Flack
                  DRUMS OF PASSION, Olatunji

176   Feelings   See page 205, Body Awareness and Feelings, 10

178   Scarf Game with Partners

                  MAN OF LA MANCHA
                  ZORBA THE GREEK

180   Newspaper

                  Any soundtrack with a variety of moods and beat such as:
                  CLOCKWORK ORANGE
                  DANCEPIECES: *In the Upper Room,* Philip Glass
                  HOOKED ON CLASSICS
                  MAN OF LA MANCHA

181   Newspaper, cleanup

                  FLASH DANCE
                  ROCKY III: *Eye Of The Tiger*
                  ZORBA THE GREEK

182   Ropes

                  CHARIOTS OF FIRE
                  DIANA ROSS' GREATEST HITS: *Reach Out And Touch*
                  FORBIDDEN OVERTURES (See listing on p. 203 to order)
                  SILK ROAD SUITE, Kitaro
                  SOUNDS OF SILENCE: *Sounds Of Silence,* Simon and Garfunkel
                  Rimsky-Korsakov, *Scheherazade: The Sea And The Boat Of Sinbad*

184   Shadow Play

                  AUTUMN and/or DECEMBER, George Winston
                  CAVERNA MAGICA, Andreas Vollenweider
                  Haydn, *Flute Quartet, Opus 5*

Additional Resources from Zephyr Press

A MOVING EXPERIENCE: THE VIDEO
by Teresa Benzwie

In this outstanding video, Benzwie guides her kindergarten students through many of the activities from the book using motion and imagination.

30-minute video (VHS format) and 8-page guide.
ZV01-W . . . $29.95

EDUCATION IN MOTION
A Practical Guide to Whole-Brain
Body Integration for Everyone
by Carla Hannaford, Cherokee Shaner, and Sandra Zachary

Promote whole-brain and body integration with researched and tested exercises. *Education in Motion* introduces you to the practical benefits of kinesiology (the study of the principles of mechanics and anatomy in relation to human movement). Watch the video for clearly demonstrated exercises to—

* Increase learning
* Improve self-esteem
* Build critical thinking skills
* Enhance communication skills
* Realize full creative potential

30-minute VHS video.
ZV03-W . . . $49

KINETIC KALEIDOSCOPE
Activities for Exploring Movement
and Energy in the Visual Arts
by Gail Neary Herman, Ph.D., and Patricia Hollingsworth, Ed.D.

These kinesthetic activities involve whole-body movement, music and rhythm, and drama. In one lesson students listen and move to the beat of the "talking drum." Then they look at rhythm in paintings and "draw" and write rhythms.

You'll get—
* A rationale for kinesthetic learning
* 12 multimodal art activities that include background, a lesson with teaching suggestions, journal writing, and a drawing or other art activity
* Introduction to kinetic energy in art, mind, voice, and movement
* More than 50 movement, art, and journal activities with background information and detailed directions
* 45 black-and-white art reproductions that relate to the lessons

Grades 3–8.
104 pages, 8 1/2" x 11", softbound.
ZB25-W . . . $20

MAPPING INNER SPACE
Learning and Teaching Mind Mapping
by Nancy Margulies

Mind mapping is a significant advance over traditional, linear note taking. Use mind mapping for personal note taking, in curriculum planning, in group process in the classroom, and as a teaching strategy in daily lessons.

Using a mind map, you can record more information on a page and show relationships among various concepts.

Mind mapping integrates the processes of both sides of the brain—the linear left side and the global right side.

For teachers of K–Adult.
128 pages, 11" x 8 1/2", softbound.
ZB18-W . . . $24.95

RHYTHMS OF LEARNING
Creative Tools for Developing Lifelong Skills
by Don G. Campbell and Chris Boyd Brewer

Here are more than 75 classroom activities to boost learning and provide opportunities for personal growth.

Learn about the physical and emotional highs and lows to promote a learning environment that is less stressful and more focused. Specific activities for teachers precede and complement the student activities.

You can—
* Discover the best learning modes of your students
* Learn to use music, art, movement, and drama to promote optimal learning states
* Use effective rhythms of presentation in your teaching
* Learn about and use the methods of Lozanov and Tomatis and the techniques of accelerated learning

Grades K–Adult.
320 pages, 7" x 9", softbound.
ZB21-W . . . $24.95

To order, write or call—

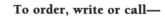

Zephyr Press
P.O. Box 66006-W
Tucson, Arizona 85728-6006
Phone—(602) 322-5090
FAX—(602) 323-9402

Please add 10% for shipping and handling costs to all orders.

You can also request a free copy of our current catalog showing other learning materials that foster whole-brain learning, creative thinking, and self-awareness.